Praise for *It All Starts with Marketing*

"Dr. Ann Marie Gorczyca is a class-act orthodontist all around. In her book, she shows it well with clever tips, proven methods of patient care, and ideas to assist in overall dental excellence all so generously shared here *to help others* become more successful and to *WOW!* their patients. She has gathered together many 'extras' one can do in the daily business of dentistry to influence and please patients, their families, their referring specialists and the community at large. What a gift to a new doctor wanting to generate happy patients and future referrals."

Rosemary Bray,
Speaker, Trainer and Consultant to the Dental and Orthodontic Profession

"What an incredible resource for dental GP's and specialists alike. Marketing is an essential ingredient for every dental practice in today's marketplace. This book fills the knowledge gap that most of us have on how to successfully market and attract new patients."

Lee Ann Brady D.M.D.,
Speaker, Dentist, Desert Sun Smiles, Glendale, Arizona

"The world of dentistry has become increasingly competitive over the past decade as marketing strategies become more and more sophisticated. Dr. Ann Marie Gorczyca has answered the need for a straight-forward, common-sense approach to marketing that any dentist can implement easily and successfully. This publication deserves the attention of all who want to continue to grow and thrive in today's professional marketplace."

Dr. Michael Cohen D.D.S.,M.S.D.,
Periodontist, Founder, The Seattle Study Club

"Dr. Ann Marie Gorczyca has a passion for business concepts and strategies as they apply to the dental world. This book is filled with many 'Why didn't I think of that first?' ideas, that are sure to help your practice grow and thrive, even in a challenging economic climate. This book will serve as an invaluable resource with diverse and easy-to-implement marketing ideas, solid advice and proven strategies for strengthening and growing your dental or specialty practice."

Maureen Valley D.M.D., M.P.H., M.S., Orthodontic Specialist,
Associate Professor, University of the Pacific,
Arthur A. Dugoni School of Dentistry

"This is the 'Go-To' marketing manual for dentists and dental specialists! It's packed with marketing tips that really work specifically for the dental practice!"

Judy Kay Mausolf,
Coach, Speaker, Author & Practice Riser

"Without question, this book is a requirement for every dentist and dental specialist determined to build an elite practice."

Neal D. Kravitz D.M.D., M.S.,
Kravitz Orthodontics, South Riding, Virginia

"Dr. Ann Marie Gorczyca started an orthodontic practice, in a competitive market, from scratch. She was determined to succeed and she has. In this book, she shares her many thoughts and ideas that took a start-up practice to the thriving practice that defines her success. This book is a fresh and energetic look into marketing with concepts that apply directly to dentistry. Marketing is perhaps the most important management aspect of starting, growing and maintaining a successful and vibrant dental practice."

Jay Wirig, Managing Partner,
Thomas, Wirig, Doll, CPAs to Dentists and Physicians

"This book is filled with simple ideas you can implement today, whether you are a new or established dental practice owner or in general or specialist practice. Dr. Gorczyca helps you think about the total care of your patients and why they entrust it with you."

James Goolnik B.D.S., M.Sc.,
Dentist and Author of "Brush," London, England

IT ALL STARTS WITH
MARKETING

201 MARKETING TIPS FOR
GROWING A DENTAL PRACTICE

DR. ANN MARIE GORCZYCA

AUTHORITY
PUBLISHING

It All Starts with Marketing: 201 Tips for Growing a Dental Practice
By Ann Marie Gorczyca

1. MED016090 – Medical: Dentistry - Practice Management
2. MED016000 – Medical: Dentistry – General
3. BUS043000 – Business & Economics: Marketing - General

ISBN: 978-1-935953-56-2

Cover design by Lewis Agrell
Interior design by Stephanie Martindale

Printed in the United States of America

Authority Publishing
11230 Gold Express Dr. #310-413
Gold River, CA 95670
800-877-1097
www.AuthorityPublishing.com

To my father, Fryderyk,
    who always encouraged me to write a book.

To my husband, Richard,
    with much love and admiration.

To my son, Richard Fryderyk,
    the joy of my life.

CONTENTS

Foreword ix

Introduction xi

How to Use This Book xv

Part One: Internal Marketing 1

    Chapter 1: Place: Your Patient Experience 3

    Chapter 2: Product: Things Patients Love 21

    Chapter 3: Price: "I Can Afford Dental Care" 43

    Chapter 4: Promotion: the Patients, the Team,
        the Doctor 47

Part Two: External Marketing: Public Relations 53

    Chapter 5: Any Time, Any Place 55

    Chapter 6: Brand 65

    Chapter 7: Communication 79

    Chapter 8: Discovery 83

    Chapter 9: Experience 95

Part Three: Relationships 101

    Chapter 10: Educate 103

    Chapter 11: Communicate 113

    Chapter 12: Participate 117

    Chapter 13: Give 121

    Chapter 14: Produce 131

Conclusion 137

Appendix 1: Marketing Calendar Template 139

Appendix 2: Sample Marketing Calendar 140

Acknowledgements 141

Index 143

About the Author 153

Bibliography 155

FOREWORD

by Fred Joyal

This book is truly about abundance. Not only is it filled to bursting with concise, unique ideas, it reveals a vision of the dental profession in which patients, colleagues and the world in general are all made better by sharing and caring about each other.

In reading Dr. Gorczyca's book, I'm reminded of how dentists are essentially practical scientists, going through their days in a very methodical way. And what Ann Marie has done here is taken that scientific approach and applied it brilliantly to dental practice marketing.

This book is a step-by-step guide to creating and implementing a well-executed marketing plan. And just as in your dentistry practice, you will find that you may make modifications and focus on some aspects more than others, and also make adjustments based on your patient base. But the whole toolkit is here, a fabulous resource that will have a profound effect on your success and the day-to-day enjoyment of your practice.

Dr. Gorczyca also reminds me of why I'm so passionate about the dental industry, because she exemplifies the quality that I see in the best dentists I know. That quality is an attitude of abundance. She is not only passionate about offering the highest quality of care to her patients, but she wants to share the keys to her success with each of her peers.

This attitude, this worldview of abundance, doesn't happen that often, in my experience. Most people are gravely concerned that there isn't enough of everything to go around, and so are extremely cautious about what they share. They guard their "secrets" closely, wary of competition, dreading failure or even just diminished wealth.

Not Ann Marie. Every conversation I've had with her has been about the advancement of the dental profession, how much opportunity there is for everyone in her field, and how every dentist can enjoy life and be more productive.

I hesitate even to call this a book, because it is more than that. It is a manual, a guidebook to success that is in small part educational and in large part practical. Some of these tips may take you a few minutes to implement, and others may take you the entire course of your practice life to perfect. But if you apply just 10% of them, you'll be 100% better off.

And that enrichment will not just be financial. You will have a happier team, a more enjoyable place to go every day, and a host of patients whose smiles you can be proud of. More than that, you will be a true professional, with a high and well-deserved standing in your community.

And you will have proven Ann Marie's greatest message: When you live from abundance, abundance comes to you. The map is right here in your hands, so let the great journey begin.

Fred Joyal
Author of *Everything is Marketing* and co-founder of 1-800-DENTIST®

INTRODUCTION

Either write something worth reading or
do something worth writing.

–Benjamin Franklin

The business of dentistry is more competitive than ever. When I opened my orthodontic practice in Northern California almost 20 years ago, there were 42 dentists in East Contra Costa County. Now there are over 100. At that time, there were only five orthodontists in the area. Now there are more than a dozen, not to mention a large discount clinic down the street and dentists who do specialist procedures. The current dental environment is changing for all of us. We can all benefit from additional resources to help us deal with the new economy. Marketing will help you embrace and conquer this challenge.

Marketing is a difficult subject for dentists to discuss. Dentistry is made up of highly educated, scientific and artistic professionals. We are a sophisticated, ethical, and sometimes shy group of individuals. Marketing is something we may wish to avoid, but we cannot. Remember that even professionalism is a form of marketing. For *everyone* running a successful dental practice, marketing is therefore an important element of the business management mix. Growth now is more dependent than ever on awareness, organization and implementation of marketing skills. Marketing is essential for dentists to survive and thrive in the new economy.

Marketing is not about marketing secrets, insider clubs or consultants who share clandestine ideas. If your marketing is not remarkable, visible to all, and known by everyone in your community—including your competition down the street—then it is probably not effective. Marketing is here for all of us to share. The biggest secret to successful marketing is taking the time to develop an effective, consistent and expeditiously executed marketing plan.

When I was a student at Harvard School of Dental Medicine, I had the opportunity to study at Harvard School of Public Health in the Department of Health Management and Policy. There, I attended my first marketing lectures and started to understand the importance and broad-reaching effects of marketing in the healthcare industry. I learned that marketing involves many things, including case studies, comparisons, differentiation, product analysis, demographics, communities and target audiences. Marketing is about personal preferences, branding and customer service. Marketing is the ability to move others and direct them toward what we have to offer – dentistry. This perspective is valuable to you, the dental professional, in the marketing of your business, your dental practice.

Like some of you, I started an orthodontic office from scratch in a new community. At first, I was a total stranger. This was very difficult, and after three months, I remember being in tears thinking that perhaps I would fail. But, due to marketing, patients quickly found their way to my door. For dental specialists, marketing is even more essential, considering that it becomes necessary to rebuild your practice with new patients after the completion of each and every case.

As a child, I loved my orthodontist and his office. It may surprise you that what impressed me most was his fish tank. Yes, that's right, his fish tank. I tell this story only to emphasize that the special things about your dental practice are what patients love and remember most about you and their experience in your office. These extraordinary things create patient experience and patient happiness. Truly magical things make a difference. They make you remarkable. All of these amazing things are marketing. When it comes to marketing, everything counts.

Included in this book are some ideas, experiences and strategies I used to gain new patients and grow my practice from the ground up. I hope that several of these tips will be helpful to you, especially those of you just starting out who may need a little help, encouragement, a positive push or a "you-can-do-it" cheer to make you feel more empowered to persevere. I hope this book is also useful to those who have been in practice for several years; those of you who are looking for a few new ideas to help make your patients feel special, your team more engaged and your office just a little more fun.

As the economy and dentistry continue to evolve, so does the marketing mix of possibilities for your dental practice. You will find that your marketing plan will need constant updating and revision to remain effective. One simple marketing truth remains: The goal of marketing is to make your phone ring and bring new patients to your front door.

I hope you'll enjoy the suggestions, stories and tips in this book. Not every idea will fit every dentist. Depending on your personality, style, brand and community, some will appeal to you, while others will not. What's important is to create happiness in your patients, community and referring doctors, as well as in you and your dental team.

When it comes to marketing, everything counts. As you're about to see, it all starts with marketing. Let's get started.

HOW TO USE THIS BOOK

If I read a book that cost me $20 and I get one good idea,
I have gotten one of the greatest bargains of all time.
                                                    –Tom Peters

What is dental marketing? Dental marketing is everything you do that has anything to do with your dental practice. Everything counts. This book outlines 201 marketing tips I have taken from my private orthodontic practice, marketing education and activity and involvement in the dental community and academia spanning 30 years. I have included what works. I have not included what I have found not to work.

Dental marketing can be divided into three main categories:

I.   Internal Marketing – Marketing to past, present and future patients, their families and friends.

II. External Marketing – Marketing to members of the community in which we practice dentistry. External marketing may also be called public relations.

III. Relationship Marketing – Marketing to dentists and physicians who refer their patients directly to our dental practices.

The aim of marketing is to make selling superfluous.
–Peter Drucker

What business are dentists in? Yes, all dentists work in a business within the healthcare industry. We are delivering dental health. We are delivering the messages, "We will take great care of you" and "You will be happy and have a better life after receiving dental treatment."

The ultimate goal of our marketing efforts each and every time is to have the phone ring with a new patient calling to schedule their initial exam. Once you understand that you are in a business, the nature of the business and how marketing fits, the marketing opportunities will naturally surface.

Each and every day you strive to restore your patients to ideal dental health. Accompanying you on this journey are the principles of dental marketing. Before patients arrive at your office, they would have heard about you, seen a reference to your office, or been referred to your office. This is done by marketing. In growing your dental practice, it all starts with marketing.

Strategy is a process, not an event.
–Mark Faust

As you read the marketing tips presented in this book, you will be able to construct your own 12-month marketing calendar (a copy can be found in the appendix). Choose 12 items from each of the book's three parts: Internal Marketing; External Marketing: Public Relations; and External Marketing: Relationships. Some items may take more than one month to complete, or be repeated more than one time. Write the date of project initiation on the calendar. Try to start three projects per month, one from each marketing category.

Once you have launched your annual marketing plan, keep track of new-patient results from each tip. Some projects may take three efforts or three months to see results. Be patient. Once you have reviewed and analyzed your results, document the winners and double your efforts in that area. Eliminate the losers and replace them with new ideas. *Carpe diem.*

Part One

INTERNAL MARKETING

If you have more money than brains you should focus on outbound marketing. If you have more brains than money, you should focus on inbound marketing.

–Guy Kawasaki

Internal marketing within the dental office is marketing to your patients—past, present and future. Internal marketing is perhaps the most powerful marketing tool for the growth of your practice and the acquisition of new patients. After a few years in practice, your number one new-patient referral source can be, should be and will be your patients.

Consider each of your patients as walking, talking billboards, spokespersons for your practice, public relations representatives and builders of relationships with your referring doctors, and watch your practice grow. The point of internal marketing is this: You want your patients to tell others, with excitement, love and enthusiasm, about you and your dental practice.

The Ps of marketing is place, product, price and promotion. Seth Godin, author of the landmark marketing book *Purple Cow* and the most popular marketing blog @ThisIsSethsBlog, adds to the Ps of marketing positioning, publicity, packaging, pass-along, permission, and "purple cow." Within internal marketing, the power is in unique, personalized promotion, in being a "purple cow," being unique, one of a kind, remarkable. This translates directly to your office feeling exceptional and being memorable.

Chapter 1

PLACE: YOUR PATIENT EXPERIENCE

*A smile is the light in your window that tells others that there is
a caring, sharing person inside.*
                                                              −Denis Waitley

What feeling does your office communicate? Does it express cheer, happiness, warmth, fun and excitement? Does your office make your patients feel well cared for, loved and special?

New patients will make a judgment about your office within the first seven seconds of entering. Visually, the office must be attractive and appealing, and the actions, words and experiences must convince the patient that they want to be there. Maintenance of your office environment may be as important as the doctor's diagnosis and treatment plan. Here are a few suggestions for patient communication, both verbal and nonverbal, to create a welcoming and remarkable office environment.

1. We Will Take Great Care of You

If you are just starting out or want to grow your current dental practice, focus your marketing efforts on the new patient experience first and clinical procedures second. "We will take great care of you" is the dental team's verbal promise and testimonial to the new patient. Tell your new patients that you will take great care of them.

One way you can show new patients that you will take great care of them is to *listen* to them. Ask new patients questions about themselves.

Devote time and attention to their responses. Care enough to listen. You want your new patient to say, "She really listened to me. She really cares."

In addition to listening, there are other things you can do to make your patients feel and trust that you will take great care of them. Be genuinely interested in your patients. Remember their name and use it often. Ask about their family and interests. Make new patients feel important. Smile.

If you are a specialist, praise the general dentist who referred the patient. Tell the patient that their dentist is the best. Tell the general dentist that you will take great care of their patient. Tell your patients that you love your office and that you are proud of the excellent dental care that you provide, your outstanding team, and the fun experience that patients have in your office. Tell and show your patient through your actions and words that you *will take great care* of them.

Nurses presently are the most trusted healthcare providers in the United States. When you observed a nurse bedside, she is most often focused on the needs and comfort of the patient, listening to them and responding to the patient's requests. Many top hospitals emphasize a "Patients First" policy of focusing on the patient above everything else and reassuring them through words and actions. Just before leaving for the operating room, my husband, a cancer surgeon, makes a point of reassuring the patient and family by simply saying "We will take great care of you."

Try telling your patients "We will take great care of you." The effect of these seven little words is amazing.

2. PATIENTS: MODELS OF CLINICAL EXCELLENCE

Your patients are walking, talking models of your clinical excellence. Your customer service and patient experience inspire your patients to talk about you and recommend you to others. This becomes your word-of-mouth marketing. Turn your patients into goodwill ambassadors of your dental practice. You would like each of your patients to tell family, friends and members of the community to come to your office for treatment.

Make it a daily habit to ask your patients for referrals. "We'd love to have more patients just like you. We love new patients! Thank you for referring your family and friends." Treating your patients well through clinical excellence, outstanding customer service and a great patient experience is the most powerful dental marketing tool you'll ever have. Provide clinical excellence and treat your patients well and they will be your top referral source.

Marketing cannot overcome poor practice habits. That you are a competent dentist is assumed. Marketing distinguishes you among a crowded field of well-trained colleagues. Marketing will take you to the next level.

3. Patient's Happiness

Honor the patient's happiness within your office and during treatment. In an orthodontic office, for example, don't remove the appliances or complete treatment until your patient is 100% satisfied with the treatment outcome. In this effort, I recommend using a Braces Removal Request Form, which states "I am happy with my orthodontic result and I am requesting removal of my braces." Not only will you document that the patient is happy with their orthodontic treatment results, but this will serve as a reference years from now should the patient not wear their retainers and state that they were not happy at the time the braces were removed.

Honor patient satisfaction. Guarantee satisfaction and the quality of your dental treatment, and redo all treatment at no charge should there be any difficulty. This will be time and money well spent in the growth of your good reputation and your practice.

4. Office Tour

Just as you would welcome a new friend to your home, you will want to welcome the new patient to your practice. This includes a welcome and guidance of the new patient through your office environment. Our office tour has nine steps:

- Warm welcome (#5)
- Refreshments, movie, magazines (#8, 9)
- Wonderful team "Wall of Fame" (#11)
- Exceptional doctor "Wall of Fame" (#12)
- Patient "Walls of Fame" (#13)
- Digital X-rays (#14)
- Brushing stations, whitening (#15)
- Seating for family and friends (#18)
- "We will take great care of you." (#1)

The office tour takes training and practice. Every team member in your office, including the doctor, should be able to give the office tour with enthusiasm.

5. WARM WELCOME

As soon as the new patient and their family arrive at your office, you can politely acknowledge them with a warm welcome. In daily preparation for this to occur, have the new-patient exam times and names posted at the station of the front office greeter. The office greeter is usually seated closest to the entrance. This advance preparation will ensure that the greeting is planned and will occur. New patients are best welcomed by name by an assigned team member, who will stand to greet the new patient and their family. The office greeter can then offer coffee or refreshments, ask what movie the new patient would like to watch or what magazine they would like to read, and give the office tour. During the office tour, a warm welcome should be given by all team members when they see the new patient and their family. During the office tour, team members will smile, take time to say hello and welcome the new patient to the office.

6. Welcome Folder

The most important aspect of the welcome folder is that it says "Welcome!" The welcome folder is a beautiful assortment of materials, which the new patient may read when they are initially seated in your office before their appointment begins. The quality of the folder reflects the quality of your office. It includes useful information about treatment, a brochure describing the office, information about the doctor's credentials, an invitation to the next patient appreciation party, as well as a list of features about what makes the doctor and office staff special. The office greeter can have all welcome folders for the day prepared at the front desk before new patients arrive. As the greeter stands and greets the new patient, she can hand the new patient the welcome folder.

7. Office Brochures

Within the welcome folder is the office brochure. The office brochure cover displays a color photo of treated patients and answers the question, "What's in it for me?" The office brochure also contains photos of the team, the doctor, the doctor's family, and the office. It lists pertinent information about the doctor's experience, training, skills and offerings in order to build credibility. Within the brochure, the core values of the office can also be listed.

Office brochures are critical for patient education, community public relations, referring doctor information and patient referral. The office should never be without a full supply of office brochures. Such color brochures produced in a quantity of one thousand can cost less than one dollar per unit.

8. Refreshments

Who doesn't love coffee? Welcome refreshments will instantly make your office a pleasant place to visit. A fresh cup of coffee, tea or hot chocolate will give patients an immediate feeling of comfort, like a tiny little vacation every time they come into your office. I highly recommend the Keurig® beverage maker, which brews fresh beverages within for individualized cups. The Keurig® machine system gives your patients the choice of coffee, tea or hot chocolate. Bottled waters and juices may also be served in the refreshment area. Cookies, muffins, cupcakes or other snacks can also be served.

If you are located in a professional building, a refreshment area will welcome referring doctors and their team members to your office for an occasional break. We have a tradition at Gorczyca Orthodontics of "Serving up the Café Mocha" and refreshments during the last day and hour of our work week. This is a nice way to end the day and say "Thank You" to our patient families. Whipped cream is sure to put a smile on everyone's face.

9. Movies and Games

Kids love funny movies. By playing the most popular new feature in your reception room, any time waiting for appointments will pass quickly and unnoticed. Patients and parents will be engaged, entertained, and relaxed, rather than gathering at the front desk, talking loudly and focusing on the time. Those in the reception area will be engrossed in the cool new movie and your reception room will be a calm, inviting, quiet and happy place.

Video games also are entertaining for young siblings and children who may accompany a brother, sister or parent for their appointment. Both movies and video games will make your office fun and will make kids look forward to returning to your reception room. These children will tell their family and friends about the cool games and movies in your dental office and the great time they had there. Parents of patients often tell me about the cool games and movies they still remember about their orthodontist's office when they were a kid.

10. Magazines

It is important to have a variety of great magazines in your office, tailored for children, teens, women and men. Men read magazines, too, and often fathers will bring their children for their appointments. *Cycling* and *Sports Illustrated* are fantastic magazines for men. Women may enjoy beautiful magazines such as *Martha Stewart* or *Oprah*. Kids enjoy *Teen Beat* and *Seventeen* magazines. And everyone enjoys look-ing at *People* magazine, which is the most popular—you can tell by the migration of this magazine in the hands of patients from the reception room to the treatment area.

Magazines can be straightened periodically during the day, at lunch-time, and at the end of the day to keep the magazine area looking clean and organized. Magazines also can be refreshed at a minimum of once per month to reflect that your dental office stays current, pays attention to detail, and cares about patient comfort and interests.

Pay close attention to the articles in your magazines and especially those listed on the cover. Be sure to have G-rated magazines with positive, beautiful content. Your magazine area and these publications you choose will be making a first impression on new patients and their families.

You may want to place an attractive label that describes your prac-tice, website, and contact information on the front of each magazine. That way, should a magazine "wander" from your office, it could still perform a "marketing" service in its new location.

11. Team "Wall of Fame"

All of your wonderful team members can have their individual photos framed, labeled with name and job title, and on display in your dental office. This gives the new patient confidence that these team members have tenure and pride in your dental office and in their work. Individual team member photos reflect the commitment that each team member has made to the patient, patient care, the office, the doctor and their team.

When describing the Team "Wall of Fame" on your new-patient office tour, compliment your team, the doctor and individual team members. You can discuss individual team member's longevity and total team experience, which added together may equal over 100 years.

12. Doctor "Wall of Fame"

The doctor's diplomas and distinctions can be displayed in the office in the new exam area where new patients and their families can easily see them. Important diplomas and distinctions can be pointed out to the new patient during the office tour. It is nice to include a family photo of the doctor to reflect the doctor's personal life. This will help to build trust with new patients and their families. The Doctor "Wall of Fame" will promote credibility with new patients, giving the message that this doctor is an accomplished, loving person who will take great care of them.

During the training process of my own team, I discovered that our team members needed to be educated about what makes their doctor unique and what makes our office remarkable and distinctive. Don't expect others to learn it or know it on their own. Explain your most valued accomplishments to them and tell them what it means to your patients. Tell your team what is extraordinary about you and your dental services, above and beyond the usual training programs.

In my own case, beyond being a Diplomate of the American Board of Orthodontics, I am proud to have served the ADA in the writing of the National Board Part II Orthodontic/Pediatric Exam Questions for a five-year period. I was honored to be the first woman accepted to the Northern California Angle Society of Orthodontists. Our office is devoted to the treatment of TMD (temporomandibular dysfunction). The diagnosis and treatment of occlusal disease is an area in which I have completed Advanced Education in Orthodontics (Roth Course) and received additional training in functional occlusion and TMD treatment. We also are leading providers in the areas of Invisalign®, orthognathic surgery, and interdisciplinary treatment. Your team needs to be informed and educated of details such as these.

13. Patient "Walls of Fame"

"A picture speaks a thousand words..." is reflected on your Patient "Walls of Fame." This may be the most important marketing feature of your dental office. Nothing will give your new patients more confidence and trust in your office, your skill, and your expertise as a dentist than seeing beautiful photos of smiling patients with excellent treatment results. Without these photos, your treatment is theoretical. The wall photos bring the theory to vibrant life. In your exam room, throughout the office, or in the X-ray area, have natural smile photos where new patients can see them and envision themselves with that same gorgeous new smile. I have actually had parents at an initial exam look at our patient "Wall of Fame" photos showcasing our great orthodontic results and say, "We want that one!"

Photos of amazing treatment results can be easily made into canvas wall hangings, which look attractive and are very reasonably priced. If you take final records, you can use your final patient smile photo. If you need final photos of patients for this purpose, you could schedule a VIP patient party, hire a photographer, and get all the photos at that time. If you schedule such a photo shoot, you may want to bring a smartphone and record some great patient testimonials at the same time.

The use of patient photos for the Patient "Walls of Fame," social media, and other forms of marketing requires patient consent. Consent can be acquired from every patient by including this agreement in the initial informed consent signed by each patient in your office.

14. Digital X-rays and Technology

New technology can benefit your patients by making their dental treatments easier, more comfortable, safer and more efficient. You can point out all of the new equipment in your office and describe how it improves patient care. In general dentistry, the CEREC machine, facilitating in-office crown fabrication in one office visit seems to have the biggest buzz. In periodontal care, the Yag laser is an excellent adjunct for gingivectomy. Microscopes facilitate endodontic treatment. Digital X-rays are low radiation. Scanners can facilitate 3D images for treatment planning. AcceleDent is a new product just out in orthodontics. All of these features deserve special attention. Acquisition of new equipment and office upgrades can be sharable and exciting office news.

15. Brushing Stations

Point out that your office has multiple tooth-brushing stations with single-use, pre-pasted toothbrushes, floss and mouthwash. You can say, "This is where you will be brushing your teeth" during the new-patient office tour. At this point, the patient is starting to imagine being a patient in your office.

Brushing stations need to remain immaculately clean while being used by your patients all day. Assign one team member to brushing station maintenance to be sure that the brushing stations are clear of cups, paper towels and ready for the office tour throughout the day.

16. CLEANLINESS

Cleanliness is the first step of new patient preparedness. Take time to make the office spotless and display the excellence of your continual maintenance. This will be the first impression that new patients have of your professionalism, attention to detail and the environment in which they will receive their dental care. Your office cleanliness is a reflection of the skill and attention to detail by you and your team.

Don't forget to check the cleanliness of the patient restroom. It should be spotless, with towels stocked, and sinks, toilets, and floors clean. Be sure to check the bathrooms a minimum of once daily.

Offices are best cleaned nightly by a professional janitorial service. Detailed cleaning and organization can be done annually or biannually by the entire team. Have the rugs cleaned at least once a year. Divide the office into distinct areas and assign individual team members to a specific area for office cleanliness responsibility. This will ensure that your office always remains spotless.

17. WHITENING

A beautiful straight, white smile is awesome. That is, after all, our ultimate goal. Tell patients that you would like them to have the whitest, brightest, most beautiful smile. Whitening is the service that can achieve this for them. Shade diagnosis can be done at the initial exam and throughout treatment. We recommend keeping the Treswhite whitening trays by Ultradent on permanent display for use for tooth whitening. For orthodontic patients, Ortho Treswhite is also available for whitening during orthodontic treatment. Whitening can also be offered as a promotional. Your office could offer free whitening for new patients or free lifetime whitening for patients who are consistent and loyal with their dental appointments and who refer new patients to your office.

18. Seating for Family and Friends

As mentioned earlier, the *reception area* (waiting room), where we receive our new patients like honored guests into our home, is welcoming and spacious. We encourage patients and friends *not* to wait in the car. By providing coffee, comfortable seating, flat screens, and even making your office a wireless "hot spot" can keep your waiting room "humming." Just like a good restaurant, people associate a "busy" business environment with a high quality product for which a short "wait" is justified.

Family and friends are always welcome not only in the reception area but also in the treatment area. In orthodontics, facilitated parental communication by having them seated in the treatment area will improve patient compliance. Inviting friends to visit your office will lead to more new patients. Friends brought to your office can be given an office brochure and an invitation to return for an examination.

Be sure to also extend invitations to family and friends of your patients to attend patient appreciation party events. This will powerfully spread the good news about your practice in your community.

19. Music

Sound can put you in a good mood. Make some music! Play music that is popular, and helps your patients feel happy and relaxed. An office without music is a sterile environment. I personally cannot work without music. If the music is ever off, I tell my team that I am going to have to sing.

We play Sirius Satellite Radio in our office; it provides a vast variety of stations, commercial-free, and static-free for easy and comfortable listening. It provides a daily endless possibility of music.

20. Office Decorations

Voilà! Visual surprises reflect an exciting fun environment and the enthusiasm of your doctor and team. It adds just one more aspect of the cheer, "It's Showtime!" Like at Disneyland, everyone loves walking in a magical environment. Niemen Marcus and Target create this well due to the visual changes, stunning colors and mobiles. Similarly, your office can reflect seasonal themes in a visually pleasing way.

Patients love noticeable changes and returning patients will comment that they can't wait to see what your next decoration will be. Young children, elementary school children, middle school children and high school teens will interact with a unique environment. Your office can also have fun posters that reflect current music heartthrobs of young patients. Presently, you might consider One Direction or Taylor Swift. Change your posters every year to stay current.

Stuffed animals give your office a high-touch feeling. Cozy and cute will certainly go further with small children and their soccer moms than technology. Expressing a soft touch will make your office attractive for young patients, their siblings and children of your patients.

Pillow pets will make little kids feel great about your office. They can be hugged at appointments, making small children feel comfortable and secure. Cute stuffed monkeys that say, "I love my hygienist," or "I love my orthodontist" or "I love my dentist" send a wonderful message. Referring offices also love receiving these cute monkeys, which they can hang from a doorknob or put on a shelf.

Decorations can be changed every eight weeks and stored for reuse year after year. Most likely no one will choose your office because of your computer system but someone may choose your office because of the way decorations or a stuffed animal made them feel.

21. FRAGRANCE

How appealing and fresh is the fragrance of your office? Enter the front entrance and check the fragrance. Office preparedness *begins* with a pleasant fragrance. The moment a new patient walks into your reception room, your office needs to smell delicious, not like a sterile, antiseptic dental office of the 1950s. Instead, use air fresheners or candle aromatherapy to give your office contemporary dental "spa" feel. You can continue this theme by adding soft music or a small water fountain.

To maintain fragrance, your dental team should be encouraged to eat lunch in a break room or out of the office. When food is eaten in the reception area as during a Lunch and Learn session, be sure to have food wrappers and lunch bags discarded in the back office where the scent of food can be contained. Test for odor after lunch before new patients arrive, and spray with air freshener if necessary. Give your office the pleasant fragrance "sniff" test.

22. Patient Trust

Do new patients and their families trust that you care about them? How does your office feel to new patients, parents and family? Prior to the new patient initial exam, the doctor and treatment coordinator can take a minute to review the new patient's name, questionnaire and important personal information so that the doctor can begin the exam by welcoming the new patient by name, discussing key points of their personal information and build a connection to start a relationship. This will make your new patient happy and show that you care about them as a person. After all, your goal is to deliver happiness to the patient. Show new patients how much you care by asking them about themselves and taking the time to discuss their points of interest and concerns.

23. Before-and-After Photos

Before-and-after photos of completed cases are extraordinary marketing tools for the orthodontist or dentist. Show new patients photos of your best completed cases. Show them how these cases used to look before treatment and that this result is the beautiful new smile that the new patient will receive from your office. Showing completed cases are the best means of explaining a proposed treatment plan to a new patient. Follow this up by telling your new patient throughout this process that you will take great care of them, too.

"Before" photos can be taken of each new patient at the initial exam. Reviewing intraoral photos will help new patients tremendously in understanding and visualizing the diagnosis, dental problem and treatment plan, and how it will improve their life and appearance. Photos can be easily displayed on an iPad, which the patient can hold in their hands.

Before-and-after photos of your patient's completed treatment can also be e-mailed to the patient with a suggestion that they post their own before-and-after photos on Facebook for the world to see. Before-and-after photos can also be given to each patient in printed form upon completion of their comprehensive care. I always joke with my patients by telling them to put their before-and-after photos on their fireplace mantle and tell everyone that I am their orthodontist. The patients think I'm kidding, but I'm really not!

Before-and-after photos can also serve as a great tell-a-friend marketing tool. Why not give the patient two before-and-after photos, one for them and one that they can pass along to introduce a friend to your office? The excitement of your patient about their completed case, which they will show their family and friends, is sure to create buzz.

24. KID'S CLUB

Young children and siblings of current patients are the lifeblood of your future practice. You can encourage these young kids to become new patients by inviting them to join your practice as soon as possible. You want your office to be a friendly and inviting place for them, where they can look forward to being a patient.

You can start a seven-and-under Kid's Club for younger siblings of current patients. If you are a pediatric dentist, you may start your club at an earlier age, perhaps under three years old. When younger brothers and sisters are in the office, we invite them to join the club by having them fill out a Kid's Club postcard and fill in the date when they will turn seven years old. In return for doing this, the child can receive a prize. This pool of future patients will also receive invitations to office events and mailings, including our annual patient appreciation party. Join the club. Kid's Club membership has its privileges!

25. COMFORT BREAK

Give your patients a comfort break. This special idea came from dental marketing guru Fred Joyal, co-founder of 1-800-DENTIST® and author of the book *Everything is Marketing*. Fred suggests that during each long procedure, the patient be given a comfort break at approximately the halfway point. This is perfect for long orthodontic procedures, such as initial bondings.

Comfort can also be enhanced by placing ChapStick® on the patient's lips prior to placing the stretching cheek retractor, rubber dam or bite block during long dental procedures. Add to this a music headset and sunglasses. The patient may also watch the procedure in an overhead mirror attached to the dental light at each treatment chair or watch an overhead DVD player. A patient blanket can be added for maximum patient comfort.

26. Fond Farewell

Each day, make a special effort to thank each and every patient who chooses your office for dental care. Take the extra time to do things that make patients happy or feel appreciated. Ask them how their visit was and do something special for them during their appointment. Tell patients and their families that you will be looking forward to seeing them again at their next appointment. Give your patients a fond farewell. Until their next appointment, this will be the last impression that you leave with your patients as they walk out the door. This impression will be with them when others ask them about your office.

27. Care Calls

Showing new patients that you care about them with a pre-treatment or post-treatment care call is a powerful marketing tool. This can be done best by the doctor or it can be done by a team member. At the end of the day, take a few minutes to personally call new patients to ask how they are doing following their initial appointment. Nothing shows you care more than simply asking, "How are you?"

Care calls take just a few minutes a day. If you miss a day, keep a record and follow up the next day or as soon as possible.

28. Thank-you Notes

After treating a new patient, it is a nice gesture to send a handwritten thank-you note, thanking them for starting treatment in your office. This card can be customized to your office and signed by each member of your orthodontic team. This small gesture will show that you took the time to think about that new patient, that you welcome them, and that you value and appreciate having them as a patient in your practice.

29. PATIENT SATISFACTION SURVEY

"How are we doing?" and "How can we get better?" When it comes to winning and keeping patients, giving them dental happiness and delighting them in every way, nothing will give you more information than a well-planned system of patient feedback. A patient satisfaction survey will give you this information. Honor your patients by giving them a satisfaction questionnaire and asking them how you could improve your dental office. This is valuable feedback and the patients will give you the best and most honest suggestions on how you can improve your office.

Of all questions, the most important marketing question is, "How likely are you to refer a friend to be a patient?" We hope that we will get a "10" in this category from every patient. Review your results monthly at your team meeting. Be sure to list the name of the dentist and each team member for individualized self-improvement feedback.

I will never forget two insightful patient comments that I have received. One read, "You have no magazines for men. I suggest *Cycling.*" We immediately bought a subscription to *Cycling* magazine and gave an extra copy directly to this patient with a note of thanks. The second comment was, "Dr. Gorczyca, I love your office, but the *National Geographic* videos have got to go!" We now show only the newest #1 G-rated DVD. We change the DVD every eight weeks.

Patient satisfaction is so important that you must have a well-thought-out strategy for measuring it and putting this information to work in your dental office. In marketing, we call this the Ostrich Syndrome. And, if you are an ostrich with your head in the sand, you may get your rear kicked because you are unaware that you are lacking patient satisfaction.

30. PATIENT TESTIMONIALS

What makes you remarkable? When you have a patient who is extremely happy with your practice, who gives you an outstanding compliment or a story about their dental joy or orthodontic success, ask them to put it in writing. Ask raving fans to write five-star reviews. Publish these testimonials on your website, in your newsletter, or post them on social media. Personal stories are the best reference of your clinical excellence, outstanding customer service and great patient experience. People believe what other people say more than advertising.

What is a great patient review? Think of a testimonial as a verbal snapshot. It will show the before-and-after condition of the patient and describe their wonderful dental experience. The patient will start with their chief complaint, their feelings about their condition, the diagnosis, and how their problem was solved. The patient will end with their awesome result, thanks to the exceptional doctor and team, how incredible their treatment made them feel, and that they highly recommend your office to others.

Use your patient comments to answer questions. Collect testimonials featuring benefits and unique features of your dental office, services and procedures. Testimonials may include answers to alleviate the new patient's fears and eliminate their doubts about the benefits of your dental services.

On our website is a favorite testimonial. This is a favorite testimonial because it was written by a once unhappy mother of two of our patients that we turned into a raving fan.

"All of the dentists said I wouldn't be happy with my cosmetic results unless I got braces. Dr. Gorczyca had a plan that enabled me to get the best smile I could. She connected me with a wonderful specialist to do a laser gingivectomy. It was the first time I could see that my teeth were so amazing. The dentist said that so much thought had gone into the structure of my mouth and tooth placement that it was the best job that he had ever seen. Now for the first time in my life, I have a smile that lights up a room. Words could never express the gratitude that I have for you, Dr. Gorczyca. Thank you so much for your guidance that you gave me every step of the way. You are a truly gifted orthodontist."

Patient stories can also be very easily videotaped on a smartphone. Tell the truth, make a video, change the world. Be sure to have signed patient consent for use of testimonials. Once filmed, personal testimonials can also be transcribed and used in social media and on printed material.

31. Directions and Signage

For potential new patients contacting your office for the first time, directions are extremely important. This is also true for your website; be sure to have the office address linked to Google Maps. Be sure to have clear, scripted directions to your office from all driving directions for easy reference by your front desk team member. Review these directions with your receptionists for ease of repetition to callers. Directions are extremely important for new patients to be able to find your office for the first time.

Visible signage on your building, indicating the location of your office from the road, can only increase business and the success of new patients finding and making it to their first appointment. Try to put pictures of your building on your website and in advertising. Make your office building a community landmark.

32. Location and Parking

The busiest intersection in a well recognized building with ample parking is always ideal for practice growth. Great freeway access and easy moving traffic is a consideration for patients and their families when initially choosing a dental office. Being next door to a middle school or high school will allow some patients to walk to their appointment after school. Your location is important for visibility, top of mind, and top of choice. If you are going to build a new office, whether you're alone, in a complex or in a large professional building, try to be on ground level so that you can get the attention of the passersby. If you are going to go to a commercial center, pick the area that has the most foot traffic. As they say in real estate, location, location, location. Use it to your benefit.

Parking is also a major consideration for patient convenience. Be sure to reserve ample parking close to the front door for your patients by you and your team members parking farthest from the entrance. You could also have some fun with parking by having a "Patient of the Month," "Team Member of the Month," or "I Got My Braces On Today" or "I Got My Braces Off Today" special VIP parking space with stand-up signage.

Chapter 2

PRODUCT: THINGS PATIENTS LOVE

To love what you do and feel that it matters—
how could anything be more fun?
–Katherine Graham

In dentistry, your main product is your patient's beautiful and healthy smile. But there are other important items for your office to give patients, and patients may love these things as much as their dental procedure. These products are important for getting patients to refer new patients to your office because they represent outstanding customer service and a great patient experience.

In creating outstanding customer service and a great patient experience, there are many things that you can implement in your dental office. These are the things that patients love. First and foremost is having fun. Institutionalize fun in your dental office. Put it in the job description. Team members that are fun, smile and laugh while getting their job done will spread their joy to your patients.

Imagine your patient saying to you, "Make me feel special." Described next are many ways to make your patients feel special. The simplest way is to say, "You are special to us." Other ways include events, recognition and gifts.

EVENTS

Those who love what they do
don't have to work a day in their lives.
                                    –Dave Kerpen

Holding events is one of the best ways to grow your dental practice. Patient appreciation events are a core element of marketing and public relations in the community. These events give the dentist and dental practice an opportunity to show their personal side, friendliness and generosity. It also gives the dentist an opportunity to meet new people and mingle with patients, community members and referring doctors. Additional family members, friends and colleagues of your current patients can in turn give a strong word-of-mouth referral of your practice at an office event.

33. KID'S DAY!

Imagine that it is a weekday civic holiday. Girls and boys are home from school and driving Mom crazy. What's a mom to do? Go to Kid's Day at Gorczyca Orthodontics!

There is nothing a mother loves more than having her child happy and seeing her child smile. Moms are in a constant quest to create happiness for their children and an event that can create this is well worth it. Contact your local company for inflatable slides and jumps and set up a play date at your office.

Kids love Jumpy Jumps. Slides are even better. Throw in a few fun games like "Who Can Jump the Longest?" or Diary of a Wimpy Kid's "Touch the Cheese" foot race and the kids will be in heaven. If set up in your office parking lot, you may want to take out a one-day insurance policy to protect yourself against general liability. Blow-up jumps and slides are relatively inexpensive and easy to set up in your office parking lot. Announce the day. Set up balloons and signs and see what happens. Be sure to call and invite all patients in your database. This can easily be done using the Televox Housecalls system. Build it and they will come.

When it comes to targeting young kids, middle school kids, teens, friends and mothers, special events are ideal. An outdoor special event will reach your audience, reach the community and often reach the media. It will also get your name out by "Word of Mom" as someone who does nice things for kids and their families.

34. SUMMER SPLASH PARTY

The Summer Splash Party is an annual tradition sponsored on a Saturday night in July for all Gorczyca Orthodontics patients, parents, family and friends. In our community of Antioch, California, there is a wonderful water park that is open for private Saturday night buy-out sales throughout the summer. The cost of this event is $1,800 for a park maximum of 1,800 people. That's $1 per person. The return on investment (ROI) is extremely good if only six new patients come from this event. In orthodontics, that would be $36,000.

The Summer Splash Party has been held by Gorczyca Orthodontics for almost two decades. It has become a community landmark and favored event. It's even better if you can get park exclusivity and have the park run announcements about your office throughout the summer. The Prewett Water Park in Antioch has seven swimming pools, hot dog stands, volleyball courts, and many other fun activities for children, parents, patients and friends. The Summer Splash Party has become our most popular event that we look forward to each and every year.

35. ICE CREAM SOCIAL

Everyone loves ice cream on a hot summer day. An ice-cream social is a fun event that can be held outdoors in your office parking lot. Ice cream vendors are available to deliver ice cream either in tubs for scooping or wrapped, which is the easiest and cleanest. Should you host an ice cream social, be aware that ice cream melts quickly in the hot sun. Have someone monitor entry into and out of your office for use of restroom facilities to prevent ice cream handprints on your doors and counters. Have hand wipes available for hand washing prior to entry into your office building.

It is fun to provide a little entertainment at your ice cream event. Children's entertainers include clowns, jugglers, dog shows, zoo shows, puppet shows, face painters and balloon sculptors. Choose a time of year that is warm but not too hot to help with the comfort of the guests and maintenance of the ice cream.

36. HALLOWEEN SKATING PARTY

A dress-up Halloween roller- or ice-skating party is a fun event that you can host for your patients, their families and friends. Local skate rinks are happy to provide a buy-out package for a one-night event. The capacity of a skate rink may, however, be smaller than an outdoor event. Our local roller rink's maximum capacity is 350.

Bowling at a local bowling alley could also be considered as a Halloween dress-up fun event. Here also, there will be a maximum capacity of how many bowlers could bowl at once. Movie theatre buy-outs may be larger. Be creative. As long as the kids get to wear their Halloween costumes and have a little activity or entertainment, they will be very happy!

37. SANTA CLAUS PARTY

A Christmas party, holiday party or Santa Claus Party is a fun event that you can hold in your office. The appearance of Santa and the opportunity to take photos with him is always a big draw for families. A well-decorated Santa Claus Party requires planning and clean up. A seasonal theme such as Halloween or Christmas may also exclude some patients who do not celebrate or recognize these holidays. Choose your seasonal holidays wisely to reflect the cultural diversity of your community.

38. HOUSE CALLS

What's the most valuable thing in your office? It may just be your phone database of all patients past, present and future. A service that has the ability to call every patient in your database, allows you to reach all of your patients at a moment's notice. This can be done at a relatively low cost. In our practice we use TeleVox HouseCalls. This service is also available from Sesame Communications. Mass database phone calls are a powerful marketing channel.

The marketing effectiveness of a patient appreciation event begins with house calls. A recorded message is made by the doctor, personally inviting every patient in the database. This process alone makes your office phone ring off the hook. If you don't have a patient appreciation party, you may want to consider a greeting or message to be sent out to all patients in your database at least once a year, perhaps during the end-of-year holiday season. Patients who have completed treatment years ago will be moved by your thoughtfulness. Should patients or their family or friends need additional services, they are more likely to call after this friendly reminder. House calls are guaranteed to create a burst of new patient exams for your office.

39. Adult Patient/Seniors Day

It's not 65 and older, it's 55+ and better! Working, stay-at-home, and retired adults are doing their own thing. They may not want to be seen at 4 p.m. after school surrounded by a room of children. Why not schedule one day per month as an adult-only day? Cater to adults and seniors and have a party. This allows you time, focus, conversation, education, and special attention for your adult and senior patients. Make your office a place where a 40+-year-old would be extremely comfortable receiving treatment. This day could also include additional information about adult orthodontics and Invisalign treatment, whitening, or implants. Challenging interdisciplinary adult orthodontic cases and orthognathic surgery cases also need additional appointment time in the orthodontic office. An adult-only day will allow you to provide this high level of care to adults with a little extra time for tender loving care. After all, TLC is TCB (Tender Loving Care is Taking Care of Business!).

40. Invisalign Day

For orthodontic specialists, you can have an annual special Invisalign Day to allow you to focus attention on spreading the word about Invisalign to patient families, the community and referring doctors. This special marketing effort can make you the Premier Provider in your area and gain you recognition on the Invisalign company website. Time and effort placed on promoting a specialized treatment, such as Invisalign, or other specialty procedures helps to build that aspect of your practice and gets people thinking and talking about your office and that special service. Your product rep can contribute to making your special day a big success by being there, bringing promotional items, and bringing food.

Begin the promotion of your special day 90 days prior to the event. Don't give up your commitment to this project even if the initial response is silence. People often wait until the very last minute to respond and partake in special events. I'll never forget our very first Invisalign Day. We had promoted the event widely in the community, with referring doctors, with patients and parents, with beauty salons, and colleges nearby. Our Invisalign rep was coming and she was committed to bringing the food. One day before, we had very few R.S.V.Ps. We almost cancelled but decided we would not because we had made a commitment and we were going to see it through. As it turned out, we started 12 new cases that day. We had many phone calls and many walk-ins, and our busiest time was between 4:00 p.m. to 5:00 p.m. that day. We scheduled overflow patients to the following days. Our very first Invisalign Day was a big success.

Starts for a special event day can be increased by a special offer for patients who start treatment on that day. These offers could include a product such as whitening or an electric toothbrush, cash savings on the treatment itself, or some other incentive reward. Be creative. Whatever you do, make your special day fun and have enthusiasm for your services and product. In return, your enthusiasm will be spread by your new patients throughout the community.

41. SUPER-START DAY

For busy families with working parents who commute hours from your community for work, a Super-Start Day for orthodontists is a convenient benefit your practice can offer. Schedule one day per month as a Super-Start Day and make it an all-inclusive day. The initial exam, records and braces can be placed the same day, minimizing the days parents need to take off work. A Super-Start Day can be done for any multistep dental procedure. The first day of the month is best for arranging Super-Start Day since the patient will need a larger down payment for multiple procedures and this usually works well with work schedules.

42. New Technology Day

If there is a revolutionary new technology that you have added to your office, set up a special day to promote and feature this new system. For me, the hottest new thing right now is AcceleDent accelerated orthodontic treatment enhanced by 20 minutes per day of electromagnetic pulsation. There are dozens of new products and equipment to choose from. Anything new is news.

Try a promotional sale of the new product to get the community to try it. We once had a Damon Braces Day to let the community know that we also carried Damon braces. That day we discounted Damon braces. As a result, we started 17 new patients in one day. To date, this is still our biggest production day in the history of our practice.

43. Debond Day

Everyone loves a party and to celebrate, especially when they are getting their braces off in the orthodontic office. One day each month we have a Debond Day and a party for all our patients getting their braces off. We sing songs (check out Gorczyca Orthodontics "Your Braces Are Off" song written by Rosemary Bray on YouTube), eat popcorn, give a candy reward, and take pictures. We also ask for reviews and testimonials on Debond Day, as well as for new patient referrals.

Debond Day can be the happiest day of the month. To create such happiness in your office, the doctor, manager and team must be involved in the idea of producing happiness. In this way you will work toward outstanding customer service, taking great care of your patients and having fun, which will ultimately produce a great patient experience.

Debond Day is a great time to ask happy, satisfied and excited patients for referrals. You may want to give patients a "Debond Gift Card" to give to a friend for use when they start orthodontic treatment in your office. You can practice your referral requests and have them scripted. Ours goes like this, "We'd love to have more patients just like you. Thank you for referring your family and friends."

OTHER EVENTS

There are many other events that can be held to market your practice. Other ideas I have not included are to rent out the local movie theater. Mini golf courses are also possible to rent out for an office event.

Renting a facility outside your office has the benefit of minimal time away from your office. Supplemental single-day insurance is not critical since an out-of-office location will already have liability coverage. Once you have found an office event that works for you, stick with it. You will become known throughout the community for that event, and patients and friends will look forward to your event, year after year.

44. OFFICE BANNER

Whenever you hold an event, especially if it is outside of your office, be sure to have your practice name clearly and openly displayed and accessible to visitors. One way this can be done is with an office banner. These are relatively inexpensive, easily made, and can be used over and over again. They are portable and reusable. They can be brought to each and every event outside of your office, whether at a school, park or PTA meeting. They can be used at all fun events to spread the name of your office. On the day of the event, it is also possible to add a standup sign for placement on the sidewalk or parking lot entrance to announce your event.

RECOGNITION

45. PERSONALIZED THANK YOU NOTES

A handwritten personalized thank you can be given to every family who refers a new patient to your office, as well as to every new patient who starts treatment in your office. The doctor and team can also take the time to offer thanks in person at the time of the next office visit.

Thank-you cards can be signed by every team member and stored by your treatment coordinator for timely use. These cards can read: "Thank you for your referral", "Thank you for choosing our office", "Thank you for referring your family and friends," and "We love patients just like you."

46. ARTICLES AND CARDS

Should you see a newspaper article about your patient having won an award or sporting event, write a personal note of congratulations mailed with the article. This note can be signed by the doctor and the entire team. You may also want to keep the entire newspaper to give to the patient at their next appointment. Patients featured in the newspaper would often like an extra copy to pass on to family and friends.

Cards may also be sent acknowledging major life events such as college, graduation, marriage or loss of a loved one. These prove that you "care enough to send the very best." Sympathy cards are highly appreciated. Remember, professionalism is the highest form of marketing. Patients and their parents will appreciate this gesture of interest and kindness.

47. CHILDREN'S PARENT RECOGNITION

Giving recognition to parents is always appreciated. One way this can be done is to ask children to write a thank-you note to their parents to be mailed from your office for something the parents have done. At our office, we do this once orthodontic treatment is completed. Children can thank their parents for the orthodontic treatment that they received. Another form of parent recognition is an essay contest for the best essay written by a child, "Why my mother is the best" or "Why my father is the best."

48. AWARDS

Awards are a joyful surprise. When a patient does something extra special in support of your office, give them recognition in the form of an award. Perhaps a patient or parent has given you outstanding office advice that has improved your office or made you more prominent in the community. These are raving fans deserving of an award for their service. Perhaps a patient has referred three patients to your office in one month. Perhaps a parent has brought multiple children to your office for treatment. Perhaps a foster parent has brought many foster children to your office for treatment. These are extraordinary people. Knowing these amazing people is a blessing and a pleasure.

You have outstanding patients and outstanding parents in your office who love you, do nice things for you and deserve recognition. Give them abundant praise in the form of awards such as "Patient of the Month," "Patient of the Year," "Parent of the Month," or "Parent of the Year." These times will be practice highlights.

49. Hygiene Certificates

Hygiene certificates are a way to involve both the patient and the hygienist in the pursuit of excellent oral hygiene. These customized office diplomas are given to patients to take to their dental cleaning appointment for documentation of good hygiene, recognition and reward. Tokens are given for the grade of excellent. Should the patient have ideal hygiene, they can receive two extra tokens. This is also an effective way to communicate with the patient's hygienist and let her know that she is important, appreciated and a member of your team.

50. 10-year Retainer Check

I once attended a lecture at the Northern California Angle Society of Orthodontists given by the former President of the American Board of Orthodontics, Dr. Raymond M. Sugiyama. He presented beautifully treated cases 30 years, 20 years and 10 years after orthodontic treatment, demonstrating perfect stability of excellent orthodontic results. After hearing his lecture, I decided to send out 10-year retainer-check postcards asking my patients, "Have you been wearing your retainer?" and telling them, "Your orthodontist cares." The result was a wonderful reunion with former patients who still looked amazing several years after completion of treatment. A few of these patients needed new retainers or minor orthodontic treatment. More surprising was that many of these patients who completed treatment 10 years ago brought in their seven-year-old children for an orthodontic evaluation! One of our team goals is to have happy, well-treated patients for life. The 10-, 20-, 30-year retainer-check program ensures that we reach that goal.

51. Keep in Touch

Keep in touch with all patients, even those who have completed active treatment such as endodontic treatment, oral surgery or orthodontic treatment completed several years ago. Make your patients "patients for life" and keep in touch. Your patients will always remain a valuable referral sources. Children of patients will be seen for initial exams once your patients have been out of orthodontic treatment for more than 10 years, since they were teens. Soon you will be treating the next generation.

The easiest way to keep in touch is to invite all of the patients in your database to your annual patient appreciation party. Sending out your recorded message is an extremely time- and cost-effective means of personally saying "hello". The patients will enjoy hearing the doctor's voice, the event given for them, and knowing that they were remembered.

Gifts

Whatever you call them, gifts or giveaways, a dental convention would not be a dental convention without them. The best booths have the best goodies, from diamond lanyards to glow in the dark mouse pads, kaleidoscope commuter mugs, to light-up lip gloss. If you give something away that is remarkable, you will long be remembered for it and people may flock to you to receive their special prize.

Such gifts are thank-you tokens from your office. One way of delivering patient happiness is to give objects of appreciation. This is another way to make patients feel special. Anyway you look at it, gifts are good.

Everyone loves surprises, especially when it comes gorgeously wrapped in beautiful paper with a colorful ribbon or in a gift basket with multicolored tissue paper sticking out. If you want to thank a patient and their family for choosing your office, give them a gift. Patients always love to be rewarded. In return, they will be happy to promote your office. Here are a few whimsical ideas of tokens of appreciation.

52. Light-up Toothbrushes

Light-up toothbrushes are exciting. A light show of these custom brushes in a basket are without a doubt the number one most remembered display patients, schools, clubs and businesses can receive from your office. These unbelievable toothbrushes are incredibly popular. When we deliver them to schools and hand them out at talks, teachers from neighboring classrooms actually come next door to ask if they can have some for themselves, family, friends and their classroom. Kids love them. Light-up toothbrushes have an internal timer to help the patient complete the ideal duration of tooth brushing. With the lights off, using this light-up toothbrush could actually make tooth brushing pretty exciting. These customized toothbrushes are available in quantities of 2,000 from www.ParadiseDentalSupplies.com.

53. Wooden Tokens

Have you ever seen how excited a kid gets to receive the tokens at Chuck E. Cheese's? Wooden tokens are a collectable item, a small gold star of appreciation for the patient coming in on time and maintaining excellent oral hygiene. In orthodontics, tokens are also given for having no appliances broken or loose. Additional tokens are given for wearing their practice T-shirt or referring a friend to your practice. Once a patient has acquired 20 tokens in an orthodontic office, this qualifies them to pick from a collection of office prizes. For children, prizes may include books, games, dolls and Legos. For adults, gift cards to local *cafés*, ice cream shops, stores or movie theatres are appreciated.

Patients may receive two tokens per appointment, one for cooperation/participation and one for wearing the customized T-shirt. A patient may also receive two tokens for referring a friend to your practice who starts treatment, or for maintaining excellent oral hygiene at their hygiene appointment with the hygienist. Adults want tokens or prizes, too! Indeed, it was an adult who asked us to be included in the wooden token program.

54. PATIENT LOGO T-SHIRTS

James Dean, Marlon Brando and Steve Jobs are famous for an American fashion statement—the simple short or long sleeved T-shirt. Dean created a level of T-shirt hipness unwitnessed before. Marlon Brando made the T-shirt cool. Steve Jobs made black an icon color and the long sleeve comfort turtle neck a fashion statement.

Search your own closets. How many T-shirts do you own? Purchased or given, most have a destination, business or event imprint. Our favorite T-shirts are faded, have holes, and may be stained or worn so thin that they resemble a piece of lingerie. T-shirts bring back memories and are comfortable and our favorite "hang out" clothing in our lives.

Would your patients wear your office T-shirt? Is your dental office T-shirt worthy? If patients love your practice, they will wear your T-shirt and become walking dental billboards. Wearing your office T-shirt to their appointments makes it pretty cool to talk about your office in the community. It's amazing to see your reception room filled with patients all wearing your office T-shirts. This becomes the atmosphere of an office rock concert! Thank your patients for wearing your office T-shirt to their appointments. Tell them they look cool. Take your patient's photo and post it on Facebook. Ask them how they like your office in their own words and then write something special about them on your Facebook page with a photo of them wearing your office T-shirt logo.

Giving your new patients a custom T-shirt at their initial appointment is a memorable gift that opens up the conversation about your office. It makes the person who receives it feel accepted and important to your office, part of your family and part of your team.

Make sure your logo shirts are stylish, hip and ageless. The simple white T-shirt with the symbols "I (heart) NY" is the most popular T-shirt in the world. Our boys/men's shirts are gray with black three-quarter-length sleeves modeled after baseball shirts. These are popular and we get many requests for additional shirts for a spouse or for donation to sports teams. We recommend black T-shirts. Black is a very popular hip color which is also popular with all types of men ranging from Harley-Davidson riders to Steve Jobs. For girls/women, we have black T-shirts with our silver sparkle logo GO for Gorczyca Orthodontics modeled after

Bebe design. Wearing a logo T-shirt to appointments can be rewarded with wooden tokens which can be collected and redeemed for a prize. For anyone interested, our shirts are customized by Monogramming by Frichy, Brentwood, Northern California (sales@frichy.com).

55. A Promotional Hat

While caps are popular among all ages, those 45 and older are most likely to wear one. Caps appeal to all income groups, but those earning between $50K and $100K own the most hats. So, if you're looking for a good office gift for successful men, this could be it.

Hats with logos are billboards in the community and constant reminders of your existence. Baseball type caps can be given to patients or worn by the dentist and the dental team. Caps are popular, especially in the hot California sun. Hats are also very popular in cold climates and can be knit and logo'd. Hats perhaps won't start a new case on their own, but a branded hat conversation can lead new patients to your dental office front door.

56. Contests

Curiosity engages both the young and old. Asking a question is just one more thing you can do to produce interest in your office. "Who Do You Love to Hug?" is one question you could ask to start a contest. Holding it on Facebook will spread your name through your patients' community of friends to help you to acquire more Likes. Family, friends and relatives can "Like" your office page and vote. Winners can be picked and you can give a cool prize.

Art contests are especially popular with little kids. You might consider "Design Dr.'s Nascar" or a simple seasonal theme. As my seven-year-old son would say "Mom, make sure you keep the entries down low so kids can see them, you know, like the boxes of kids cereal and toys in the supermarket!"

Pumpkin decorating contests are a thrill at Halloween. Carved pumpkins last a short time, maybe two days. It is best to have your patients drop off their pumpkins the day of the contest and pick them up later that day.

Guessing contests like "Guess the Super Bowl Score and Winner" or "Guess How Many Jelly Beans in the Jar" are easy. The possibilities are endless. Be creative and mix it up.

57. Tickets

In the San Francisco Bay Area, we love the San Francisco Giants. What could be better than a set of San Francisco Giants tickets as a big moment from your office? Tickets to local sporting events take appreciation to the next level for patients, team members and referring doctors. Should you buy season tickets to your local sports teams, in addition to enjoying the sports season yourself as a fan, you will have an ample supply of excess tickets to use for marketing.

When I married my husband 10 years ago, I gained season box seats to the San Francisco Giants. We had so many extra tickets that I just started giving them out. Suddenly, I had many new friends. It is a tremendous thrill for a child to attend a professional baseball game with their dad. I loved the thank-you notes and personal stories I received in return from my patients.

58. Electric Toothbrush/Oral Hygiene Kit

After an initial dental exam or after the initial bonding of orthodontic appliances of a new patient, an electric toothbrush and oral hygiene kit is the gift of dental oral health. Crest-Oral B offers a stunning electric toothbrush oral hygiene gift package that can be purchased and customized for your office. These kits are also useful as gifts for other promotional events in which you may be asked to participate in your community. It's always a good idea to have a few of these kits in the office at all times for use with the daily new patient or to grab when you are rushing out the door for a guest appearance at an event.

59. Treasure/Reward Chest

No dental office would be complete without a treasure chest of toys and prizes. It is an essential motivational tool for new patients under the age of nine. Children love being rewarded for a job well done at their exam. This process will create a bond with the patient and make them excited about your dental office. It will make them look forward to when they can return. If an older patient brings younger siblings to your office, or parents bring a child, ask these young children also if they would like to visit the treasure chest. In this way, you make your new patient, younger siblings, children and parents happy.

Don't forget, adults need rewards, too! It is handy to have a Reward Chest with gift cards ready for that special moment when you need to give special recognition to an adult.

60. Be the Tooth Fairy

Orthodontists, pediatric dentists and general dentists often extract primary teeth in young children. We routinely see primary teeth hanging by a periodontal thread. When we see this we help the patient with their hanging primary tooth by removing it simply, quickly and easily. At this time, you can be the Tooth Fairy. Ask the patient if they believe in the Tooth Fairy. If the patient says "yes," you can say "The Tooth Fairy left this silver dollar for you today." Have silver dollars ready in your office to give to these brave young patients.

This idea of being a Tooth Fairy was relayed to me by the parent and patient of a general dentist in my community. These patients thought their general dentist was so wonderful for being the Tooth Fairy that they could not stop raving about him in my orthodontic office. They vowed that they would refer all their family and friends to him for his Tooth Fairy kindness.

You may consider also giving adults the reward of a silver dollar from the Tooth Fairy. It's unlikely that an adult would refuse such a token after undergoing an extraction.

61. Bottled Water with Custom Labels

It's easy and inexpensive to have custom-label bottled water created as a promotional item for your office. I have seen this done at Davidson & Licht Jewelers, a very high-end jewelry store in Walnut Creek, California. Once you enter the store on a hot day, bottled water with a custom label is served on a silver platter by a white-gloved concierge. This is staged marketing theater—memorable to this day, always appreciated.

Each year for the Gorczyca Orthodontics Summer Splash Party, we distribute bottled water with custom labels. The water goes with our Splash theme. Custom labels are extremely inexpensive and easily placed over the existing label. We deliver these to referring offices and businesses in the community. Labels can also list the day and time of the upcoming event. This gift is useful and unique as well as zero calories.

62. Pens and Pencils

By now you're saying, "What's up with all the ephemera?" simply put "stuff." The possibilities are endless. Indeed, if you need additional ideas, visit the Advertising Specialty Institute at www.asicentral.com. Fear not, you're half way through. These are mentioned first because they truly are the easiest and longest lasting marketing action you could undertake immediately. They could also be the most successful.

Customized pens and pencils are the most popular promotional item in the world. You simply cannot have enough pens and pencils. Writing instruments consist of 50% of promotional products received in the U.S. Your pens and pencils will be found everywhere spread far and wide from your office by you, your team and your patients. You will find your office pens and pencils in a 50-mile radius from your office. City offices in our city have our pens. Schools have our pencils. Waitresses wear our pens in their aprons and spread them to customers signing their checks. If you need just one office promotional item in your office to get started, this is it.

To emphasize the power of such a small item as a pencil, let me tell you an interesting family story. My mother was principal of an elementary school that had a bookstore. One year, the bookstore pencil order had a big error. Instead of ordering a gross of pencils, 12 X 12 or 144 pencils, they mistakenly ordered a gross of gross, that is 144 x 144 or 20,736 pencils! These pencils were already custom engraved with the name of the school and could not be returned. So, making the best of the situation, my mother decided to have a school wide pencil sale. Every child in the school sold 50 pencils in a fundraiser. The school earned a lot of money, which enabled them to fund an innovative "International Year" of education and learning about international cultures. Every child in the school had their nationality represented in visiting presentations of art, poetry, song or dance. For this program, my mother received many civic awards. Then the program received national acclaim, the school became recognized as a National School of Excellence, and featured in an article in the publication *U.S. News* and *World Report*! Walking down the street for the Fourth of July fireworks with my mother that year, I could not help but notice that absolutely everyone in the city of her elementary school knew her! It can be the same for you and your dental office. Never underestimate the power of a pencil!

63. WRISTBANDS

Nike had an idea. They would make a special "Livestrong" Baller Band to raise money for the Lance Armstrong Foundation. They hoped to sell 5 million for $1 each. They ended up selling 85 million. Bright yellow, these wristbands are easily seen and last forever. What Armstrong's agent had first called a "stupid idea" turned out to be a big success.

Cool things for a child include wristbands. Kids collect them. I often see patients come in with 10 wristbands, five on each wrist. Mylar bands are the most sparkling and economical choice. These bracelets are the clip-together type given at amusement parks and rock concerts. Customized, they come in a variety of beautiful, vivid colors kids love. They are eye-catching and incredibly inexpensive, about $.03 each. These can be given out to promote a special product, such as Invisalign®, and the name of your office.

Rubber bands are even more popular. Silly bands are of course fun, yet not customized. This item will do nothing to promote your practice. Aim to pick wristbands that are customized with your office logo and telephone number. Give one to each patient and then give them an extra one for a friend.

64. FRISBEES

Are Frisbees retro? Do you have a Frisbee that you've had in your garage for forty years? Frisbees never seem to go out of style. I'm sure you probably still have one from when you were a kid. We have a variety of items in our office with the yellow smiley face theme, and a customized smiley face Frisbee is one of them. Frisbees are popular at the beach, parks, outings and on the school playground. Your customized Frisbees will be everywhere and last forever.

65. CUSTOM BEACH BALLS AND TOWELS

Our annual special event is a giant pool party (#34) and custom beach balls and towels go with this theme. Balls of any kind with the name of your office will be played with by children in the community all year long and will last year after year.

Custom beach towels can also be a useful reminder of your practice. Spread out on the sand or the back of a beach chair, it is like an office banner. These towels can be used at the neighborhood pools and beaches and are blazingly obvious conversation starters.

66. REFRIGERATOR MAGNETS

How many of your friends DO NOT HAVE refrigerator magnets? Perhaps your answer is very few. Customized refrigerator magnets are collectable, cute, and a great reminder to your patient and their family of your office phone number. Visitors to the homes of your patients are also sure to see the refrigerator magnet from your office, so make them whimsical and eye-catching. Change the design each time you order. Your office presence in the kitchen will be at a very popular gathering place, the refrigerator.

67. Key Ring Lights

A real estate agent once attended one of my patient appreciation parties. As he was leaving the event he told me, "You need something like we use in real estate, a small inexpensive trinket for each guest to remember you by in case they want to call you tomorrow to schedule a new patient orthodontic exam." I asked him, "What do you recommend?" He replied "A key-ring light."

Key rings are useful. Add a light to it and they become a bit extraordinary. They can be used to help open the door of your car or home in the darkness, read a program at the theater during a performance, or at the end of a rock concert as a twinkle of light. They can even be used to look into someone's mouth in case of a dental emergency. Customized light-up key rings make a great office giveaway gift for children, teens and adults. They are small, durable, modern, popular and extremely cost effective. They get the marketing job done.

68. Calendars

Making a custom office calendar can be a great way to engage both patients and referring offices. Patients can be given blank paper with their birthday month and asked to draw a picture for your office calendar. Entries can be displayed in your office for selection. Winners can be picked for each month and their drawing placed in your calendar. Kids love to have their drawings featured. Take a picture of the monthly winner with their drawing and put it on your office Facebook page each month for a seasonal display.

Everyone loves attention and making a photo calendar is one way to give it to them. You can also make a calendar summarizing community events with photos of your patients, team members or members of the dental community. One such calendar was made by an oral surgeon in our dental community. Everyone couldn't wait to see the calendar each year with hopes of being in it. This oral surgeon was invited to each and every office event where teams hoped to be photographed and make it into next year's edition. The day the calendar was delivered, we would rush to open it and see who was featured. Phone calls would be made with comments, fun observations and news of the photos.

Magnetized calendars are a simpler, less time-consuming option. Magnetic calendars on the refrigerator can be a helpful tool in the organization of a family. These can be customized for your office and given to every patient. Magnet calendars come in a variety of beautiful scenic backgrounds from which to choose.

69. DRINKWARE

Coffee mugs, glass mugs, ice mugs and bottles are common customized branded drinkware. They can also be filled with treats, included in gift baskets, given to your patients at orthodontic debond appointments, or as a door prizes at events.

A new patient of mine once filled out the exam questionnaire and wrote, "I was referred by a sports bottle!" This mom had received a Gorczyca Orthodontics "I love braces" bottle at the Opening Day of Little League. She read the name and telephone number on the bottle as she was removing it from the dishwasher. She was reminded that she needed to make an orthodontic exam appointment. As a result of having the number in her hands in front of her, she took action. She picked up the phone, called and scheduled her new patient exam, and started orthodontic treatment in our office. Cheers!

70. POEMS, POSITIVE WORDS, TAGLINES

A poem can be a form of enlightenment or an expression of love and optimism. Poems can easily be given to your patients and their families at their dental appointment. There are many wonderful poems. A favorite of mine is "Take Home a Smile," by Edgar Guest. We often use this title as a tagline in our orthodontic office. There is no better poem for optimism than The Optimist Creed available on the Optimist website, www.optimist.org. The Optimist mission is "By providing hope and positive vision, Optimists bring out the best in kids." You can give the Optimist Creed to patients and referring dentists, as well as family and friends. I keep this poem framed on my desk and refer to it often.

Never underestimate the power of positive words. Your patients visit your office for dental treatment. Leave them with a bit of inspiration and motivation through your positive words and positive actions.

Taglines are extremely positive, meaningful and memorable. In this way, I think of them as a little bit of poetry. Taglines, like poetry, come in many forms. Here are a few forms of famous taglines with a comparison to some we have used in our orthodontic office:

The Imperative: "Feel the love" –Crocs; "Love your smile"

The Descriptive: "Ideas worth spreading" –TED; "Your smile is our inspiration"

The Superlative: "The ultimate driving machine" –BMW; "The straightest, whitest teeth"

The Provocative: "Got milk?" –Dairy Council; "Isn't it time for a beautiful smile?"

The Specific: "Happy hunting" –eBay; "Happiness is your smile"

71. Going-green Tote Bags

Congratulations! You have made it to the end of ephemera, simply put "stuff!" Perhaps you are thinking that these items are a waste of resources and polluting the environment. If so, this last item is perfect just for you.

Everyone and everything is becoming environmentally conscious or "going green." Earth Day is April 22nd. Single-use plastic bags are now being banned by many cities in California. A reusable bag has the potential to replace over 600 single-use plastic bags over its lifetime. This significantly reduces plastic bag litter and reduces the one-time use of paper bags.

You may want to become an environmentally conscious green dental office. You can get rid of plastic bags and get customized "going green" reusable tote bags for your dental patients. Customized "going green" tote bags can be useful for delivery of patient items to your patient and reused by the patient and their family for many purposes in their daily lives. For more information on how you can become a green dental office, you can visit www.ecodentistry.org.

Chapter 3

PRICE: "I CAN AFFORD DENTAL CARE"

Price is what you pay. Value is what you get.
                                    –Warren Buffett

If, after presenting the ideal comprehensive dental treatment plan to the patient, the doctor or treatment coordinator receives the reply, "It's too expensive." Consider that the patient is saying to you, "Show me how I can afford it." When attempting to deliver dental happiness to the hearts and minds of patients and their families, the first step, in these challenging economic times, is often engendering the realization that, "I can afford this dental care."

Price, financial arrangements and value are more important than ever. All the marketing in the world is useless if the patient in your office cannot afford the dental treatment and financial arrangements that you are presenting. Should the doctor and treatment coordinator receive the reply, "It's too expensive" after presenting ideal comprehensive dental treatment, consider that the patient is saying, "Show me how I can afford it." Then, make it happen.

72. EXTENDED PAYMENT PLANS

Let's face it: ideal interdisciplinary dental treatment is expensive, especially for patients who have no dental insurance. It is important to convey to the patient that value is quality over price (Value=Quality/Price). The price is usually not negotiable, but payment plans can be customized.

Should a patient need an extended payment plan to pay for current treatment, Care Credit and Springstone Financing are good financing options. With these plans, payment is made by the patient to the outside financing company over five years with a small amount of interest. The good news is that your office receives the full patient payment minus a small percentage at the start of treatment without additional hassle.

73. Insurance

To have happy patients who readily start treatment, it is helpful to bill their insurance and accept payment. This is not a recommendation to accept plans that cause the dentist to agree to a lower fee. You can provide billing and receiving the payment.

Years ago Gorczyca Orthodontics tried going insurance-free. We did this for six months. What we found was that it was more time-consuming and troublesome to be free of insurance than to accept insurance. Patients came to us with more questions about the billing and payment than before. By not having paperwork, we could not answer these questions. Being in charge of the patients' insurance billing allows you to get the job done, collect the money and provide outstanding customer service. Your office will also have payment history and information to answer the patient's questions. By billing, more patients will choose your services and be satisfied with your practice and spread the word about your office to others.

74. 0% Financing

Years ago before I opened my practice in Antioch, CA, I worked in the Orthodontic Department at the University of the Pacific Dental School in San Francisco. One of my duties was to complete initial orthodontic exams for patients seeking orthodontic treatment at the school. It was there that I notice that a large percentage of new patients came from Antioch, CA. This was very surprising to me, considering that the distance between these two locations is about a one and a half hour drive. At that time, the fees in East County were very high, and financing options were more limited. Families found it was worth a drive 50 miles to make orthodontic treatment possible.

Our office in Antioch, California now offers 0% financing for two-year orthodontic treatment. This is needed in our community. This policy makes us popular with the families we treat and has worked out well for our office and for the families we serve. It is my goal that mutually acceptable financial arrangements be created for all patients seeking treatment at our office enabling the patient to start treatment.

75. Savings

If a family is considering starting multiple family members in treatment at the same time, give them an incentive. Give them a family plan. In our office we give a 5% savings for the second immediate family member to start orthodontic treatment at the same time as another family member. This idea of a family savings could perhaps be applied to other services in dentistry. It is also possible that the down payment could be built into the payment plan for the second family member in treatment. Patient loyalty is precious and should be recognized and rewarded. We love making entire families patients of our office.

Wouldn't it be wonderful if every patient paid in full at the start of treatment? A payment-in-full savings will encourage this behavior. When patients pay in full, always give them a pre-payment courtesy savings discount.

Here's a word about sales, which can be a powerful marketing tool. Discounts are powerful. This might be the only excuse some potential buyers need to buy from you for the first time. It is possible to have a sale periodically. Nordstrom's does it. If you are the Nordstrom's or Bloomingdale's of dentistry, you can have a sale. If you are Costco or Target, you cannot.

At a recent meeting, friend of mine, Dr. Neal Kravitz, shared his philosophy regarding the question, "Can I have a discount?" His answer is, "Yes you can! If you start today and pay by cash or check your total treatment fee, including insurance, you can have a 20% discount." Insurance can later be billed and refunded to the patient. I think his response is a good one, and a 20% savings is very generous.

76. On-hold Messaging

What will new patients say about your practice? What they hear about your practice and what you tell them. One way to tell patients about your practice is on-hold messaging. This service can be provided by TeleVox or Sesame Communications. Include in your on-hold messaging whatever you would like to tell patients and what you would like them to tell others. Examples include information about the doctor, Board Certification, range of services provided, new technologies and information about office events and the team. Once put into place, on-hold messaging can usually be updated annually at no additional charge.

77. Flat-screen Announcements

A flat screen in the reception area of your office is useful for relaying current news about your office to every patient and visitor who enters. Special attention can be given to a new service, a special event you may be hosting in your practice, or breaking news. One such event could be an Invisalign® Day. Product videos could also be shown for patient education.

Dr. Maureen Valley recommends a flat screen product from the company Kaleidoscope, which she feels is cutting edge for flat screen announcements. They can be found online at www.thekaleidoscope.com.

78. Promotional E-mails

Why is e-mail so powerful? Because you can click "send" and have your message reach potentially thousands of people in an instant, and it won't cost you a penny. It's a sales channel. For this purpose, make building your e-mail list daily an office goal.

We are now dealing with the e-mail, texting, social-media generation. From cost effectiveness and time efficiency standpoint, the best way to communicate with your patients is through e-mail, text messaging and online newsletters. Invitations for events, parties or new-product announcements can be made through promotional e-mails, electronic newsletters, and social media. Constant contact is one of many potential services that can help your practice to grow in this regard.

Chapter 4

PROMOTION: THE PATIENTS, THE TEAM, THE DOCTOR

You never get a second chance to make a good first impression.
                                                    –Anonymous

Of the four Ps of marketing—place, product, price and promotion—the power is in promotion.

To the patient: Thank you for choosing our office and referring to us! We love getting new patients just like you! Thank you! Thank you! Thank you!

To the team member: If you are not happy and excited to be at work, if you do not love your patients, team and doctor, you need to go. Friendliness is the most important aspect of practice promotion. Your team will not exude friendliness without excellent attitudes and a joy for work.

To the doctor: No one is going to promote your dental practice the way you will. You are the leader. You set the tone. You lead by example. You are, after all, the person patients come to see. The team may change, the cases may be completed, but you will always be there, carrying on, promoting your practice each and every day.

79. THANKS

When was the last time you thanked a patient for choosing your office? Was it a few hours ago? Today? Last week? Last month? It is not possible to thank patients enough for choosing your office, talking about your office or referring to your office. Thank you starts the conversation. You can continue by asking, "Is there anything more we can do for you?" Once you get the "thank you" conversation going, you can also ask, "How are we doing?" Listen. Improve.

80. EXCELLENT TEAM ATTITUDE

Each team member, especially the doctor, should choose to have an excellent attitude each and every day. An excellent attitude is one of teamwork, enthusiasm, gratitude and service to the patient. It is also important for making the office fun and a great work environment. An excellent attitude is essential for creating an awesome patient experience.

As a team, you are responsible for encouraging the best attitudes in each other. There are many things you and your team can do to instantly improve team attitude. Many offices start the day by saying, "It's Showtime!" Our office says, "Great patient opportunity today!" You could simply say, "Go Team!" or "It's a great day!"

Choose team members with outstanding attitudes. You can always teach skill, but you cannot teach attitude. Be sure to avoid what Stephen R. Covey called "The cancers of attitude— complaining, criticizing, comparing, competing and contending." If you have someone with a bad attitude on your team, you will never regret when they leave, only that they stayed too long.

81. PROFESSIONAL DRESS AND DEMEANOR

Being good in both image and action is the first step of being self-confident and successful. Your appearance, body language and verbal skills are important. This is the first impression of you to your patients. You want it to be professional. If "It's Showtime," everyone needs to look and be at their best. You only get one chance to make a good first impression. Your image as a dental healthcare provider is clean, trustworthy, and healthy. How others perceive you is crucial to your business success.

Uniforms accomplish the goal of professional dress. They often include monogrammed shirts with your office name and logo. These can be provided by the office with a different color for each day of the work week. Individuals can provide their own white or khaki slacks and professional shoes. Be sure to have shoes clean and polished, pants hemmed, hygienic appearance, well-groomed hair and straight white teeth. Pay careful attention to appearance. An easy way to see what your patients see is to take a picture and evaluate how you look yourself. What could you improve?

The dentist especially needs to be well-dressed. A white embroidered doctor jacket always looks sharp when treating patients. If you put pens in your top pocket, make sure they don't bleed. Doctor scrubs do not look as attractive as a shirt and tie. Our office actually took a patient survey to ask about professional dress preference and our patients answered that they preferred not to see scrubs.

During cooler months, team jackets are useful to wear to and from the office. Running errands after work, everyone will be meeting a lot of new people in the community. Noticing the jacket logo, new acquaintances and friends will make comments and ask questions about your office. Jackets are also good for teamwork and morale. As in sports, a team uniform and team jacket builds unity. Members can also carry their personal business cards in their pocket so that at special times like these, direct referrals can easily be made.

One evening after a day at Gorczyca Orthodontics, I went to the local grocery store to pick up some food for my family's dinner. It was autumn and a bit chilly, so I grabbed a Gorczyca Orthodontics logo'd team jacket to wear as I was leaving the office. As I checked out my groceries, the cashier looked at my jacket and said "Gorczyca Orthodontics. I've been meaning to call Dr. Gorczyca. Can you tell me about her?" So I told her about myself and the clinical excellence, outstanding customer service and great patient experience that we provide for our patients at Gorczyca Orthodontics. Then I told her I was Dr. Gorczyca and we had a laugh. These random personal interactions sparked by a casual glance at a logo'd jacket make for great new patient relations. This effect is what our dental marketing is all about.

Within the office, new acquaintances and patients will have a first impression of you and your team within seven seconds of meeting you or entering your office front door for their first time. Use choice words and language and express caring and kind actions. Ask a lot of questions. Show that you care. Actions that are polite and well-behaved will build trust and foster respect for your office.

To maintain a high standard, have a team code of business etiquette in professional dress and demeanor clearly written in the Team Handbook. Review it regularly and reinforce it. A unified team is professional in dress and demeanor and wears them with pride. Plan to update and replace your team uniforms and doctor jackets regularly. I once asked a "Cast member" at Disneyland how it was that everyone there looked so good. She replied, "It's easy. If we don't look great, we get sent home."

Be sure to enforce your high standards in dress and demeanor and do everything you can to achieve them. I once bought my treatment coordinator a new black suit and Ivanka Trump blank pumps. She looked great! Everyone noticed what a big difference that one change in dress made in her attitude, in her interactions with others, and in her effectiveness as a team member. She was now dressed for success. If you or someone on your team would benefit from a professional image make-over, consider contacting the Image Expert, Janice Hurley-Trailor at www.janicehurleytrailor.com. Take time to visit her website to get ideas and see her results. Janice makes her clients look gorgeous.

82. Team Business Cards

Each person in your office would love to have a personalized business card. This is tangible evidence that you value this person in your practice as part of your team. Business cards relay a sign of permanence. Personalized cards also help patients remember their favorite assistant, especially those needed to speak a foreign language. We include "Se habla espanol" on the cards of those who speak Spanish, which is a tool for outreach to the Hispanic community.

How thrilling for a new team member to receive her personalized business cards for the first time. She feels a sense of professionalism, respect, belonging and is proud. She rushes home and gives out cards to her family and friends. Her parents are proud and hand out her cards to other family members and friends.

Business cards are also handy to give to patients who ask for them. Assistants can ask patients to personally call them if they have any additional questions about the office or the treatment they received at their visit that day. Business cards reflect ownership in the patient experience.

Team members can give happy patients two personal business cards, one for the patient and one for a friend, and tell the patient that the practice would love to have more incredible patients just like them. Cards can be kept in the treatment area for easy access. What an incredible value for less than $100 for 1,000 business cards, or less than 10 cents per card for a referral.

Everyone who works in the dental office is a professional and deserves a business card. Cards reflect all job descriptions and titles. They can be kept in wallets or in cars. Periodically at an office meeting, you can randomly ask for business cards to ensure that everyone is supplied and well-stocked. You can even create a contest and see who can give out the most office business cards to new patients in the community each month. Give a prize!

83. Smiling Doctor, Friendly Team

Friendliness can best be expressed by a smile. The #1 marketing attribute that will grow your dental practice is friendliness. Friendliness begins with the doctor and is expressed by each member of your team. If you see the doctor or someone on your team in a grumpy mood, tell them to "Turn that frown upside down!" and "Smile!" Be lighthearted and make it a goal to give patients a reason to smile at each and every appointment. Make the doctor the smile captain. Make sure your patients take home a smile. Make your patient's day with a friendly and enjoyable office visit.

Happiness is an office culture that needs to be a top priority. Joy cannot exist without excellent teamwork based on trust, communication, commitment, accountability, results and excellence. Everyone benefits from a happy office environment.

Not everyone is naturally cheerful and happy. One of the best marketing decisions you could ever make is to only maintain "Good Apples" on your team. Hopefully your office seeks and selects happy people when hiring new team members. If you have one unhappy "Bad Apple" on your team, it can spoil the whole bunch. A person who is unfriendly, self-centered or negative can reduce the joy of the patients, team, doctor and everyone around them. You will never regret eliminating a bad apple influence from your office as quickly as possible.

84. ELEVATOR PITCH

The dentist and the team must know, believe and live by the office's core values. The elevator pitch is a concise metaphorical equivalent of your core values; a description of your office that is so compelling that the person you're with wants to hear still more when the elevator door opens. These can take 30 seconds to recite and can be practiced by everyone who works in the office. Preparation comes in handy when someone you randomly meet says, "Tell me about your office." Out comes your business focus simply stated. Make it short, smooth, compelling and understandable, even by a child.

At Gorczyca Orthodontics, our core values are clinical excellence, outstanding customer service and a great patient experience. Recently, we added a fourth item, good value, meaning that the cost of treatment in our office is well worth it. These values are written in our handbook, reviewed routinely and memorized.

What if you had to condense your core values to one word, a single one-word pitch? What would yours be? Ours is excellence. This is our brand. It is our one-word equity.

Part Two

EXTERNAL MARKETING: PUBLIC RELATIONS

"I'm a great dentist" –Marketing
"I'm just the right dentist for you" –Advertising
"I understand you're a great dentist" –Branding
"Trust me, he's a great dentist." –Public Relations
–Dr. James Goolnik

External marketing includes all exposure of the doctor, team and dental practice in the community. This exposure can include visibility at schools, community centers, businesses, speaker events and the Internet.

Public relations should be distinguished from publicity when it comes to healthcare. In medicine, it is commonly said that "There is no such thing as good publicity." Instead, what you are aiming for is good public relations.

Public relations encompasses community involvement, publicity, business affiliations, events and memberships. It is a marketing method that should be considered for the exposure, name recognition, trust and credibility it can give. Public relations is the key to dental practice success. Demonstrate your conscientiousness with your good deeds and good works in the community and be a giving place. Affiliations are public relations, so choose wisely.

Public relations can be further defined as the following: an ongoing conversation that builds a relationship between your practice and the public, resulting in influence and action. That action will be having the phone ring with a new patient.

Make community participation a dental team sport. Ask each team member to become involved in five activities a year. In Antioch, California, there are 116 annual events planned listed in our community

Welcome Guide. It is not possible to participate each and every time but certainly showing up at one per month is a doable goal. Most of all, it is important that the dentist shows up and be a recognized figure in the community.

Patients and community are two marketing target areas that I have found can produce over 51% of your direct referrals. If you have not focused on internal marketing with your patients and external marketing directly to the community, it is possible that you have missed an additional 51% of new patients, which could have doubled your practice.

As our economy changes and fewer people in the community have dental insurance or a dentist, external marketing becomes more important in attracting new patients. In California in 2012, uninsured patients were estimated to be as high as 50% of the population. Therefore, your external marketing public relations effort needs to reach as much as 50% of the population who may need dental treatment.

Next we will explore the A, B, C, D, E of marketing: Any Time, Any Place, Brand, Communication, Discovery and Experience. The next five chapters will address each of these topics in detail.

Chapter 5

ANY TIME, ANY PLACE

New business will be won only to the extent
that the client believes that the professional is
interested, cares, and is trying to help.
                                        –David H. Maister

85. DENTAL HEALTH EVANGELIST

Have you ever seen someone in public, a total stranger with really unhealthy teeth and gums in need of dental care salvation? This person could be a workman or delivery person to your dental office or home. It could be the woman behind a café counter. It could be the relative of the person you meet at a speaking engagement who comes up to you in the parking lot asking for dental advice. Or they could be the person who hears that you are a dentist and corners you in the restroom to ask about a dental problem that they have been having.

The next time this happens to you, invite this person to your dental office for a complimentary initial exam. Save them and change the world. Have a sense of urgency about it. Be passionate about helping people achieve ideal dental health. Believe in your cause. Believe in having a positive impact and changing people's lives.

People with dental neglect either have fear of dental procedures, fear of dental cost or both. If you can build trust and help them take the first step toward restoring their dental health, you will have a wonderful patient for life who will also refer their family and friends.

The new patients saved by dental health evangelists are the $40,000+ cases. They are visible in the community right in front of you. If you meet this new patient, ask in a friendly, sincere and caring manner, "Have you ever thought of dental treatment? I can help you. Just come to my dental office for a complimentary, no-obligation examination. I will take great care of you and we will proceed at your pace, together, one step at a time." Tell the patient that they have the rest of their life to achieve ideal dental health, and that you'll take it one tooth at a time, one day at a time and one year at a time. You'll stick by them and be there for them. You will care for them. All they need to do is get started.

86. COMPLIMENTARY OR FREE CONSULTATION

There is one word that is considered to be the most powerful word in marketing—"free." In dentistry, we commonly use the word "complimentary." It is a beautiful and elegant word, bringing to mind exceptional customer service.

Some potential new patients in this day and age in America may not know the meaning of the word complimentary. Maybe we should replace the word "complimentary" with "free."

All of your dental marketing for new patients should contain this magic line: "Call, e-mail or visit today for your complimentary consultation." Free is a desired word in the language of marketing. Yet, in the language of dentistry, we prefer not to use the word "complimentary" as to not devalue our services and to sound as professional as possible. Make your own choice which word is right for you, your practice, and your community.

Once you have your new patient in your dental office, have examined them, and have explained their need for your dental services, aim for a 90% case acceptance rate. Follow up and study your conversion rate of newly examined patients into treated patients. After all, marketing is worthless if you and your team cannot successfully get the new patient to commit to the start of treatment in your office.

Before you launch your community marketing plan, review your core values one more time. What will you represent in the minds of your future patients? What benefits will you offer them? If you know the answers to these questions, your positioning will be easy to determine and your strategy easier to plan. Identify all your target markets. Then take careful aim at each.

The Big Four

Markets exist as viable target audiences for the dentist. In this chapter we will discuss schools. In the next two chapters we will discuss print, community, and the Internet.

Schools

Where do most of your new patients come from? If you're an orthodontist, pediatric dentist, oral surgeon or even a general dentist, most of your new patients are in a day-care center or at school. Most adults who want a dentist have a dentist. Therefore, schools are an important community hub for new dental patients.

What is the best method to use to offer your educational services to a school? Send a flyer. Whatever your office or business wants to offer, whether it be an event, gift or educational talk, send a flyer to all the schools within your geographical area. Then, sit back and wait for the calls to come. They will come. Offer it, print it, send it, and they will come.

87. Daycare Centers

You may want to begin your school program with day-care centers. Start young. Children need to learn how to brush their teeth and the habits of good oral hygiene as soon as they are able to hold a toothbrush. The orthodontist, pediatric dentist, dentist or dental team member can visit community day-care centers and demonstrate toothbrushing, deliver toothbrushes, tooth treasure chests and cute ice packs, sharing with the kids the fun activities and stories that kids love.

Dino the Dinosaur always accompanies Dr. Gorczyca on visits to daycare centers and school classrooms with children up to age eight. Dino has giant teeth and uses a giant toothbrush to brush his teeth. After he brushes, he swishes with water and then squirts the children with a surprise spray! This delights the children and they ask to have it repeated again and again. The children receive a customized office goody bag and handouts to take home and share with their parents. This fun and friendly oral hygiene visit makes for a memorable day.

88. ELEMENTARY SCHOOLS

With elementary school children, I usually review such hot topics as "How to Stop Thumb Sucking." "Put a Band-Aid on the finger that you suck. This usually can stop thumb sucking. If not, try dipping your finger in something that does not taste or smell good. This could be food or a prescription product. If neither of these ideas work, visit your orthodontist for a habit appliance."

Elementary school children also need to know how to remove a baby tooth. I always tell them, "Do not use the methods shown in cartoons, of tying a string around your tooth to a doorknob and shutting the door!" I wish these cartoons had never been made! Removing a wiggly tooth is very easy. Simply squeeze the tooth and twist it, like putting a key into a key lock and unlocking the door.

Teachers and students in kindergarten through second grade love a visit from the orthodontist, pediatric dentist, dentist or any team member, not to mention any stuffed animal with big teeth! The children love surprises. Become truly magical and become an overnight community star.

89. MIDDLE SCHOOLS

Capturing the attention of middle school students can be a bit challenging. Should you visit as a guest speaker, you need to add challenging educational content to capture the attention of this age group. For an orthodontist, this would include orthodontic study models and before-and-after cases.

Dental vocabulary can also be mysterious, interesting, and just pretty cool. The words I like to review are "deciduous," "succedaneus" and "malocclusion." Computer spell checks don't even know how to spell "succedaneus." I compare the primary and permanent teeth to deciduous trees and talk about that which succeeds, maladies and the word "mal" meaning bad in French. Kids and teachers are somewhat intrigued and love learning about the meaning and derivation of these new words.

Middle school students would also like to learn how to become a dentist or an orthodontist or any other career advice that you may like to give. I tell them that I wanted to be an orthodontist since I was thirteen years old and in the seventh grade. These young minds are impressionable and if inspired, career choices could be influenced by your visit.

90. DONATE BOOKS

If the orthodontist, dentist or team does not have time to visit schools or if the schools in your area do not allow educational visits by dentists, you can still participate in school programs by donating books or supplies. One possible donation is a paperback dictionary, one for every child. For grades seven and up, thesauruses may be needed. This is a rare resource material that may not be available to all students. Books can be purchased and distributed at a reasonable price.

My sister, an internal medicine physician in family practice, relayed to me that she would always keep children's books in a basket in her office. If she received a new patient who was a child, she would let them choose a book from her to keep as their own. Recently, she saw a longtime patient who told her that they still remembered twenty-five years later that she had given them that book. You probably love to read. Otherwise, you would not be reading this book! Consider sharing your love of reading with your community and your patients.

91. CAREER-DAY SPEAKER

A dentist can be an entertaining career-day speaker. To get started, create a volunteer letter and mail it to the guidance counselor at local middle schools and high schools. Then, decide how many invitations you can accept.

Veterinarians who show up with an armadillos are a hard act to follow. If you find yourself in such a group, go first. How can you be fun and interesting? Radiographs are always a crowd pleaser, especially the lateral cephalometric skull. The dental development of the primary and succedaneous dentition study model is also amazing. I share that I wanted to be an orthodontist since seventh grade, and that this is not too early in their life start thinking about what they would like to be. If they can dream it, they can be it. I tell the kids what fun we had in dental school. Wouldn't it be tremendous to be back together with your dental school gang? Consider telling the students how happy you are that you made the decision to become a dentist and what it was like to live in a dormitory and go to school until grade 23. If you elicit a few "oohs" and "ahs," you know your presentation was pretty cool.

92. Visitors

Come one, come all! Visitors welcome. Network and get your name out into the community. Field trips to your office for all ages can be arranged. Visitors may include local schools or community groups such as the Brownies, Boy Scouts or Girl Scouts. High school seniors are often looking to visit businesses during their senior year. Volunteer your office as a class office visit center and welcome the students to a career in dentistry. Another form of outreach that elicits enormous goodwill is to host groups from foster homes, adult care centers or day programs for disabled individuals. Promote good oral hygiene, explain what your practice is all about, and you just might gain a new patient or family. Do well by doing good.

93. Case Donations

Donating a case to charity is admirable. School fundraisers are my favorite way of doing free care for a good cause. Be sure to not only donate the care, but also attend the event and meet the school community. Go up on stage. Say a few words. This makes for memorable public relations.

If you are going to donate a case, clearly state that insurance cannot be billed for the donated treatment for which there will be no charge in your office. Also state that the patient needs to accept the ideal treatment plan presented by the doctor. It is possible that you could get involved in a donation case where the ideal treatment plan includes extractions, palatal expansion, or even surgery if orthodontics is involved. Should the recipient decline your ideal treatment plan, then you will still be obligated to provide the treatment which you donated and your treatment results may not reflect the standard high quality of your results. This is a risk associated with doing a donation case. Your dental results remain your permanent business card, and so, you want all of them to be to your highest standard.

Donated treatment in itself does not necessarily generate new referrals. Indeed, donated treatment is likely to generate requests for more donated treatment. Free services can also lead to high no-show rates. Case donation is an admirable way to serve the public. Be sure to manage it well and be clear about the terms and the patient's commitment to care.

94. PRINCIPAL FOR THE DAY

Should a local school have a fundraising auction and there is an auctioned experience by which the dentist could meet new people, bid for it. Principal for the Day is one such example. It is a wonderful experience to be principal for the day at your local elementary or middle school. You will visit every classroom, talk to the children about an interesting and educational topic, meet with the principal and have lunch with the teachers. It's actually a lot of fun!

You may choose to talk about dentistry or oral health, but other informative topics are also welcome. Because I am a musician, I enjoy speaking to the children about a classical music composer and listening to music with them. Whether you speak about the music of Beethoven or dentistry, having a guest visitor to the classroom is always a thrill for the kids.

95. CLASS AWARD

If you are going to make a donation to a school or give an award, consider picking a class or event before senior graduation when most recipients have their minds on the graduation party and college. Eighth grade is a fabulous award class. Middle schools have few scholarships. Be creative with your generosity. There's a whole age range of worthy achievers out there from the first day of kindergarten to the last day of senior year.

An incredible award is The Harvard Book Award, obtained from Harvard University via the local Harvard Club, given to the top student in the junior class. When I was in high school I received this award. It really meant a lot to me because it was the only award at that time. Because of that, it stood out. It was remarkable. I still cherish it to this day.

96. HOMECOMING SPONSOR

Think a yearbook ad in the local high school yearbook will get you new patients? It will not. You need to think bigger than that. A series of ads may work, but it is difficult, if not impossible, to implement a series of ads in a local high school environment.

You need to show your face at the local high school. Homecoming is a great event at which to appear. In our community, there are at least 4,000 people at the homecoming event. If you can sponsor the event with advertising in the program, participating in the parade, or even driving the Homecoming King and Queen around the football field in a convertible, by all means do it. It will lead to new patients, new patient families, and new friends in your community.

I sponsored a homecoming event once and I must admit, it was one of the most unbelievable events I ever participated in. Sharing my excitement for the upcoming day with my friend, the oral surgeon upstairs, she asked, "How can I join in?" She joined me in my red convertible. We first drove the high school principal in the pregame parade with the marching band directly behind us. Then at halftime, we drove the Homecoming King and Queen around the football field. This is what I call putting the public back in public relations!

97. PARENT TEACHER ASSOCIATIONS

Parent Teacher Associations (PTAs) are always looking for sponsors for their local meetings. Besides giving dental advice in person, invite attendees to your office, say hello, introduce yourself, and tell parents who you are, what you have to offer and how you can help their family with their dental needs. Set up a display table where you and your team can interact with parents and those in attendance. Here you can engage in four types of marketing at the same time.

1. Hand out a gift with your logo and phone number.

2. Hand out brochures.

3. Demonstrate your treatment. Display before-and-after photos. Bring study models.

4. Offer free consultations.

98. School District Events

Every year, our city's Department of Schools invites businesses to sponsor a table, make a donation, and attend the end of the year school dinner and award ceremony for teachers and administrators. It is possible that your local school district provides a similar opportunity to you, whereby you can invite five other referring dentists, business owners or parents to join you for a gala dinner. Face time with the public is inexpensive, powerful and feels great. Sponsorship is an activity from which everyone benefits.

99. Junior College Speaker

The dentist, orthodontist or other dental specialist can be a speaker at local community colleges. Whether the focus is dental-assisting, career development, or an associate's degree, such programs and students are eager and enthusiastic about receiving "real world" advice. If you have a team member who graduated from the local community college, encourage her to stay involved with the department and serve on a volunteer board for her program. Doctors may also volunteer to be the graduation speaker for the dental assisting or hygiene programs. You may also benefit from having a junior college faculty member on your local American Association of Dental Office Managers (AADOM) Advisory Board.

Chapter 6

BRAND

"For truly, I say to you,
if you have faith like a grain of mustard seed,
nothing will be impossible for you."
—Matthew 17:20

My maiden name is Gorczyca. It means "mustard seed" in Polish. It's hard to spell but easy to remember. And, there are very few names like it. I'm listed in the phone book and on the Internet by name under orthodontics and dentistry and I'm easy to find. If you find me, you will probably also see my picture.

If you are a female dentist, I highly recommend that you keep your maiden name or the name that you had in dental school for life. Life brings about a lot of changes, marriage, divorce, loss of a husband, remarriage. There's no need for you to lose your name brand identity in life. You can still use your married family name in your private life and save your maiden professional name for the office.

"It's Bond, James Bond." It's not Reliable Detective Services, or Handsome Undercover Agent. This name has meaning, branding, and so does yours. A personal name has power and represents identity. Other name brands are Martha Stewart and Oprah Winfrey. These are personal name brands and they are authentic.

Be yourself; everyone else is already taken.
                                        –Oscar Wilde

People trust brand names. Brand name awareness equals credibility. Awareness and growth of your personal brand will build confidence in it. Harry Beckwith, in his book, *Selling the Invisible,* states that at the heart of a successful service brand is the integrity of the people behind it. Personal name branding is a guarantee of satisfaction.

A dental office achieves brand recognition by repetition of its distinctive name. If you need a name for your dental office, start with your own. Use the name of the dentist. This is brand "you." Be proud of your name. Distinctive names are more apt to be remembered. Being remembered often is the key to getting new business. Share of mind equals share of market.

Repetition works. You are your story and the dental office with the best story wins. Be a rock star and make your community your stage. Stir emotion. Tell your story. Sing like Adele.

Your branding will reflect your office story. It needs to be simple, clear, distinctive and remarkable. When viewed and read, you have seven seconds of attention time before the reader moves on to the next piece of printed material. Make sure your office story is simply obvious in images and words.

Your logo symbol can be simple. Think of Target, a red dot in a red circle. Our symbol is a designed interconnecting GO for Gorczyca Orthodontics. We got this simple symbol idea from Gary Danko, rated by the Zagat Guide as the best restaurant in San Francisco. Symbols are everywhere on everything. Logotype is a word or the words in a deter-mined font. The best logotypes represent the personality of the company. Ours is in Adobe Caslon. It's straight, clean and simple, like beautiful straight teeth. Frequently, a logotype is juxtaposed with a symbol. This formal relationship is your signature. Memorable signatures are clean and have color. Ours is usually gold engraved. For us, this represents excellence and value.

The dentist's photo can also be shown over and over again until it is recognized in the community. Patient photos can also produce the effect of recognition through repetition. People in our community often comment, "Oh, you're the office with the photo of the boy and girl together in braces!"

Intentionally designing in advance your brand strategy of color, imagery, topography, and composition will make your entire marketing program cohesive and differentiated, and look and feel distinctive.

Colors change. As I write this book our office is in the process of updating our colors. We feel that adding more color sends the message that we are a fun office and that visiting us will lead to a positive outcome. Don't be afraid to experiment, but once you find a branding style that works, stick with it. Consistency matters. Refreshing and updating periodically remain important to keep the public's attention.

Next come words. Words are news, the news of your office. Your news can be your core values stated in a popular way. Simply stated, our core values are "Beautiful Straight Teeth, Great Care, Fun Experience." Our favorite tagline is "Take Home a Smile". Shorter still is a one-word pitch. Ours is "Excellence."

Your story, your most powerful brand recognition, will be defined by the emotions and experiences that you present. Don't forget a call to action. This could be "Call Today!" or "Call Now!" followed by the phone number of your dental office. Once you define your brand identity, you're ready. The key to lasting brand awareness is consistency.

100. Welcome Guide

The prime reason for using magazines as an advertising medium is the lasting value of the advertisement. Have your ad done professionally by an advertising agency. Then use this ad over and over again. You can even have a poster made of your advertisement and hang it on your office wall.

One great community magazine is a Welcome Guide that is printed once a year in many towns and cities. A Welcome Guide that lists all the events and services provided in your community is an excellent place to be listed and to be discovered by people who have just moved to town. The Welcome Guide is placed in a variety of businesses and recreation centers, and it is given to all new homeowners. These individuals will be actively looking for dental services.

Advertising in the final analysis should be news.
If it is not news, it is worthless.

–Adolph Ochs

101. COMMUNITY GUIDE

This booklet is printed quarterly and lists all schools, civic groups, Girl Scouts, Boy Scouts, Little League, groups and events in your community. It is a wonderful place to list your office with an attractive photo of you and your team. If you are going to have a listing in your Community Guide, keep it positive, short and to the point, and make people smile when they see it. Print a fun photo of a patient or your team, with your tagline, and your office information.

102. DIRECT-MAIL POSTCARDS

Direct-mail postcards can be effective for acquiring new patients. If you are going to send a direct-mail postcard, you have seven seconds to get your message across to the reader, so make your call to action brief. Have your office name and phone number clearly demarcated. For the best results, direct mailings need to be repeated a minimum of three times.

Affordable Image in Phoenix, Arizona is a very cost-effective, creative company for direct-mail postcards. They can be reached at www.affordableimagedental.com. Postcards may also be made to announce events or other campaigns your practice is hosting within your community.

103. VALPAK

You may be surprised to read this: nothing reaches most homes more effectively than ValPak. At a low cost (about $.026 per home) it is easy to reach thousands of homes in your local community. ValPak also provides online offers. An additional service of new patient phone call recording and call tracking is also provided. With this you will receive an online summary of every call made to your office from this campaign and be able to listen to the recorded initial phone calls of these new patients talking with your receptionists to schedule their initial exam in your office. This is a valuable systems management feature to help polish the skills of the receptionists in your office in their handling of the initial phone call.

The ValPak form of marketing has given us our highest marketing return on investment (ROI) over the years in our blue-collar community. In the San Francisco Bay Area, our target audience is $75,000 and above family income level. ValPak has been shown to work well with all demographics. You may want to give a special offer with an offer ending date, or a call to action.

ValPak is a valuable delivery system. What makes this system so effective is its vast distribution. A single mailing can cost effectively reach 10,000 to 50,000 or more households. If you do ValPak or any other form of print advertising, repeat the process a minimum of three times for maximum effect. Conversely, effectiveness can plateau or even diminish after six to nine repetitions without new and fresh offers.

ValPak also has many powerful Internet associations, which will make your offer visible online at minimal extra charge. Your ValPak "virtual" visibility on the Internet will draw attention. For patients who rely on the Internet for information, this ValPak campaign visibility can be reproduced instantly and spread to dozens, hundreds, or even thousands of others. This will enhance your ValPak presence virally. The association with ValPak will also improve your SEO, or search engine optimization, on the Internet.

104. CHURCH BULLETINS

If you place an advertisement in a church bulletin, there will be time for potential new patients to read it. We have all been seated at events and services where the speaker has continued on and our minds shifted to reading printed materials at hand. Your print ad in the church bulletin also shows community support from your office, which is appreciated. It also displays social values.

105. MAGAZINE ARTICLES

How do you get a magazine to write an article about you and your dental office? Call and tell the editors about a revolutionary new product you have to offer or a breakthrough technology. Be amazed about the dental treatment that you provide, enthusiastic about the hottest features of your technology, and confident about the clinical excellence of your procedures. Take the magazine publishers or staff out to lunch and share this information with them. You can also write your own article and submit it for publication. Magazines are always looking for new stories. Your article just might be the one they choose.

106. LOCAL ARTS PERFORMANCES

There are many performances and events, both artistic and cultural, that you may want to sponsor by placement of a print advertisement. These events may be the local orchestra, theatre group or dance company. Your dental or specialty office can place a "Best Wishes" message to the actors, musicians or other performers.

107. SMILE OF THE WEEK

Your local newspaper may have a weekly "Smile of the Week" program where you can enter your patients' dazzling new smiles for publication. Your patients will be excited to be entered into the newspaper contest and even more thrilled if they win. If your newspaper does not have a "Smile of the Week" section, partner with the editor and start one. It will help build their readership and garner publicity free of charge for your dental office.

108. OFFICE SIGNS: POSTERS, BANNERS, AND FLYERS

Office posters can be used over and over again for many events. You can make your own design with a picture of you and your team, or you can acquire posters from vendors, highlighting the products or services that you provide. Be sure to have your office poster placed on poster board. This can be done inexpensively at a local framing shop. The poster can then be hung on walls or placed on an easel in your building's lobby for special days, or at any and all outside events. Durable role-up banners are also convenient for a wide variety of uses.

109. SIGNS ON BULLETIN BOARDS

Should you have an event at your dental office or in the community that you are promoting, don't forget to pin up flyers on bulletin boards in your community. Jay Conrad Levenson, in his book *Guerilla Marketing*, recommends these words on signs:

Announcing, benefits, fast, free, how, now, power, sale, secrets, solution, why, yes.

Mr. Levenson also notes that Yale University psychologists tell us that the most persuasive words in the English language are:

Discovery, easy, guarantee, health, love, money, new, proven, results, safety, save, you.

Signs on bulletin boards are great because they are high visibility and no cost. I'm talking about small signs three by five inches, postcard size. Your sign could even be a colorful business card.

Where are these bulletin boards? They are in businesses, stations, bus stops, schools, senior centers, colleges, churches, community centers, apartment buildings, grocery stores, malls, cafeterias, public places, libraries, Chambers of Commerce, roller rinks, bowling alleys, waiting rooms and banks. Keep a stack of postcard signs in your briefcase or purse for easy deployment!

Don't forget local school campuses. College students are always looking for things to do in the community and they are attracted to the most powerful word in marketing, "free." Many students will already know your office or may have been former patients. They might well be encouraged to come back for your event then sign up for additional dental treatment that they may need and have been avoiding.

110. RADIO

Radio advertising would perhaps take your marketing efforts to the next level. As a multimedia form, local radio can be more powerful than the printed word in establishing relationships with healthcare consumers. There's something about hearing the doctor's voice that somehow makes the listener feel that they already know this person. This personal touch can be persuasive.

Your radio spot could cost $5 or $1,500. The types of radio stations are as varied as all of society. Record a 30-minute interview and then take out the best short "sound bites." Once you have recorded your 30-second advertisement, run it on several stations and evaluate which works best for you. Remember to use "persuasive" words, "ear" words rather than "eye" words. Music lends a powerful emotional overtone.

The best time to run your radio ad is during morning or afternoon drive time. We all listen to the radio on our commutes to and from work. I once heard a show from a local dental office in our community where the announcers were having breakfast at the dental office. Repeat your phone number at least three times. Also, mention your URL in your commercial so that listeners can easily access your website after hearing the advertisement. Ideally, it would be great to run your radio ad five times per day, four days per week, three weeks per month. Keep careful track of radio advertising effectiveness. As with all types of marketing, continue winners eliminate losers. Continue to test and fine tune your activities.

111. MAKE A VIDEO

Tell the truth. Make a video. Change the world. Today, with flip-cams and iPhones, it's easy to shoot a video and upload it yourself to the Internet. Videos could include an office tour, an introduction of the doctor, a new technology feature, a patient testimonial, or an upcoming community event sponsored by your office. Videos are a great way for your community to get to know you and what your office can provide.

It is possible to have an in-office professional video made of you and your office. There are several TV shows, such as *The Wellness Hour* with Randy Alvarez that can make a professional video or half-hour TV show for you. This video can be played as an advertisement on local cable TV in your community. The medium that still offers the largest audience when it comes to word of mouth (WOM) is still none other than television. When it comes to brand conversations, television commercials account for 11 percent of all conversations, more than Internet, at just 4.5 percent. Time watching television is still five times greater than time spent on Facebook.

Many professional dental companies or professional organizations such as the American Association of Orthodontists, also have videos that you can readily use. One of my favorite videos from the American Association of Orthodontists is, "My appearance, My smile," stating that when it comes to braces, retainers, and aligners, an orthodontist is the smart choice. Check out YouTube for the organizations that you belong to and the products that you use to see what you can find to suit your use.

COMMUNITY

The community can be divided into smaller target markets. Examples include ethnic groups, adults 55+ and women.

112. ETHNIC GROUPS

Know the ethnic groups within your community and cater to them. California is 25% Hispanic and Spanish-speaking. If you practice dentistry in California, you want to reach out to the Hispanic community and have at least one person in your office who speaks Spanish. In many communities in California, it is essential to have a Spanish-speaking assistant, receptionist and treatment coordinator, and Spanish materials that read "!Hablamos Espanol!" This includes educational materials, business cards and brochures written in Spanish. If you have secondary languages spoken in your community, be sure to have your services reflect these language needs to best welcome all cultural groups to your practice.

To reach specific groups, consider an advertising presence in ethnic newspapers, cable TV channels, and events. Many people still rely on their native language media for their news and dental health information. Also, remember to honor ethnic holidays and heroes, such as Martin Luther King Day, Black History Month, Cesar Chavez Day, and Cinco de Mayo.

113. AGE 55+

Surveys have shown that seniors 55+ rank health first in order of importance in their lives. Older people respond well to services that appeal to their long-term goals of health and independence.

Consider bringing the good news of dental health to senior groups, activities and clubs in your community. Volunteer to give a dental health talk at a retirement center. If you are going to communicate using printed materials or advertisement, use large print. Did you know that the AARP (American Association of Retired Persons) magazine has the largest circulation in the United States?

114. WOMEN

Include women as a target audience and direct marketing efforts specifically toward women. Why? Women have power. They are mothers, wives, partners, business owners and decision makers.

Jay Conrad Levenson, in his book *Guerilla Marketing*, reveals that women control the majority of purchase decisions. Women control 60% of all wealth and influence in the United States. They also handle family finances in most families. Women start companies at twice the rate of men and employ more people than the Fortune 500 companies combined.

Find local women's and mom's groups in your community. You can become involved with these groups by hosting a meeting at your dental office or becoming a guest speaker. If you are male, consider having a female member of your dental team do this outreach. When it comes to marketing to women, women want a conversation. Be ready to talk to women.

When it comes to service, no one appreciates good service more than a busy mom. Don't keep moms waiting. Quality service is even more important than price, location, convenience and selection. Moms are pinched for time with busy schedules and many responsibilities.

115. Civic Centers

We all focus on visiting our referring dentists and physicians as reminders for referrals. What about visiting a civic center? How thrilled would City Hall, the police department, fire department or the local bank be to receive a friendly hello with a cookie basket or a basket of new toothbrushes? Guess what? You will make their day! Think of your civic centers the same way you think of your referring offices. Keep public safety officers and officials in the marketing mix of important targets for future referrals.

My young son and I once visited City Hall around Christmas and delivered Christmas cookies and light-up toothbrushes. It was a big thrill for my son to visit with me and I considered him my little Christmas elf. Everywhere we visited, everyone was so happy to see us and receive a gift, especially an edible one. A few weeks later one of my patients who worked at City Hall told me she told all her co-workers "That's my orthodontist!" and that they responded, "She is so nice!"

116. Brochure Placement

Place your brochures, when possible, at community centers. These may include parks, libraries, the YMCA or gyms just to name a few. Many such locales have brochure stands and walls. Should you be a supporter of that center in some way, they will allow you to place your brochures on display at no charge. Some community organizations, clubs or businesses may charge a small fee.

117. Opening Days

There are numerous opening-day events in your community in which you can participate. Opening-day events will advertise you as a sponsor, post your office name, and publically thank you. You will also have the opportunity to publically thank the organization or the league. When it comes to advertising and sponsorship, think big. You can either sponsor an individual or a group, or you can sponsor the entire organization by sponsoring opening day.

I'll never forget sponsoring opening day of Little League in Antioch, California. The high school football stadium was totally packed. There must have been 8,000 people there. The Mayor of Antioch and I were on center field. The mayor got to throw out the opening pitch. I got to make a brief statement about good sportsmanship and teamwork. Four thousand customized water bottles were distributed to the kids on the teams. And, the mayor and I became friends.

If you hand out water bottles on opening day, you may reach 4,000 people at a cost of $1 each. This is a very low cost-per-contact. If you sponsor a team and it costs $500, and your cost spread over 20 team members is $25 per contact is high. That cost-per-contact ROI (return on investment) is high. These may be high quality contacts, with whom you plan to spend more time. Or, this may be a one-time contact. Think about your marketing ROI in terms of number of contacts, cost per contact and type of involvement. When it comes to community, invest, get involved and think big.

118. HALLOWEEN REVERSE CANVASSING

Children trick-or-treating at your team members' homes in your office community can be considered "come to me" reverse canvassing. Distributing Halloween toothbrushes from the local homes of your team members is a great way to get your name out in the community. Halloween toothbrushes are very popular because they are so unique, remarkable and necessary. They have black bristles. How spooky! Kids love using them. What could be better than a toothbrush to promote brushing after eating a Halloween chocolate?

Cute custom trick-or-treat bags with your office information can also be ordered and distributed either from your office or home. Little kids love getting them, and their parents will be happy to have something that their kids can use on Halloween night.

Some dental and orthodontic offices have Halloween candy buyback programs. These offices buy back the sugar-filled Halloween candy for $1/lb. and send it to troops overseas. This promotes dental health and is a nice socially conscious activity. If you are the first in your community to do candy buyback, it may lead to some free publicity with the local paper or TV station.

Chapter 7

COMMUNICATION

Never believe a few caring people can't change the world.
For indeed, that's all who ever have.
                                                    –Margaret Mead

You as the dentist are a business owner. Participation in local business networking groups will promote your practice with other business leaders in the community and spread the name of your office. You can also volunteer to give a talk to business groups, either on dental care procedures or on management principles of dentistry as a small business.

There are many events, meetings and forums in your community in which to communicate your message of dental health. Here are a few ideas.

119. City Council Meeting

The American Association of Orthodontists (AAO) Council of Communications suggests that orthodontists go to their city council meeting and ask the mayor to declare October National Orthodontic Health Month in the city in which they practice. I did this and it was a big hit! This gave me the opportunity to introduce myself to the city council and make a quick public statement that, "The American Association of Orthodontists recommends that each child receive an orthodontic examination by an orthodontist by age seven." This meeting was also broadcast live on cable TV. Our office received a Letter of Declaration from the mayor. At the same time, we gained a new patient, the city comptroller, who came to our office for an orthodontic evaluation, started orthodontic treatment and received interdisciplinary comprehensive treatment of a full-mouth reconstruction for severely worn teeth.

120. COMMUNITY BUSINESS NETWORK

Your community may already have a club named "Your town" Business Network. Join it. General dentists, orthodontists and dental specialists are one more valued and experienced professional to add to the mix of business owners. Participation in local networking groups will promote your practice while benefiting you and others.

Giving a talk to business groups on general dental care or dental specialty care is marketing theater staged. Talks can also be given on business management principles such as marketing, teamwork, treatment coordination (sales), customer service, management systems or human resource management. Your experience and knowledge as a dentist could be used to help others in the business world working nearby in your area. This is "win-win" networking.

121. ROTARY CLUB INTERNATIONAL

Rotary Club International is a well-known community service group. The Rotarians feature a guest speaker each week at their meeting. Any dentist can take advantage of this opportunity for outreach.

It was a wonderful experience for me to speak at the Rotary Club meeting in Antioch, California. The presentation that I gave described comprehensive interdisciplinary treatment and showed the results of implant restorations after orthodontic treatment. After the presentation, a Rotary member, a fifty-year-old businessman, husband and father, approached me and said, "Prior to hearing your talk today, I had procrastinated about my own dental implants. For years, my dentist has told me that I need to have orthodontic treatment and get dental implants for multiple missing teeth. Having heard your talk today, I am no longer scared to start this dental implant treatment. Being scared has made me avoid and procrastinate getting started. Now that I have heard and seen your presentation, I am no longer scared. I am ready to get started."

122. Chamber of Commerce

The local Chamber of Commerce is valuable community group in which dentists can network. Chambers of Commerce generally hold reception-type meetings hosted each month by a different business member at their home office. Attendees have the opportunity to introduce themselves, mingle and bring a door prize to the event. You, the dentist, as a business owner can donate a gift basket or other raffle item, mingle, and make new friends in your local community. This process will bring a lot of name recognition and goodwill to your office. You will also learn about local current events, community happenings and gain business tips as well as having a fabulous time.

123. Hospitals

Physicians are your dental healthcare colleagues. Dentists and physicians work together to achieve ideal oral systemic health. Get to know physicians and work closely with them. This can be done by speaking at hospitals about systemic dental issues. To get more involved in the oral systemic health, go to www.oralsystemicconnection.com or follow www.drdansindlar.com. Dr. Dan Sindlar is dedicated to helping dentists succeed in saving lives through oral systemic health.

If your family has unique talents that can be appreciated by your dental or medical community, have them participate as a representative of your office. My husband, an orthopaedic oncologist, has served in the American Dental Association (ADA) committee on orthopaedic implants, spoken to our local Seattle Study Club, and given grand rounds at the local hospital. I was fortunate to attend and be introduced as his wife, and an orthodontist. As a result, I have had many physicians as patients in my office after the initial connection that my husband helped to create with the medical community.

Chapter 8

DISCOVERY

Content is King!

–Bill Gates

INTERNET

Internet and social media presence are at the intersection of your patients and public relations. You will be participating in a conversation about your office. Conversations are markets and engagement is marketing. Authenticity makes you real, not just an office or a name. Expressing yourself with transparency will add credibility to your message. Use social media well and you will speak to the masses.

How will potential new patients find a new orthodontist, dentist or dental specialist? Reports have stated that 80% will use a mobile website or Internet search; 70% trust others' opinions online; 20% will call and ask questions. Only 14% or less will use the Yellow Pages. The percentage of new patients using the Internet grows higher and higher every day. In this day and age, the Internet needs to be a major player in your marketing mix, if not your top priority.

124. YOUR PRIMARY WEBSITE

Can new patients schedule exams on your website? Does your website answer immediately who you are and what services you offer? In five seconds, your website should answer the question "Why am I here?" You want the reader to schedule an appointment and say:

I want dentistry

I want braces, Invisalign®, retainers

I want dental specialty services

I want an initial exam

Your website can show your services and products to the public. Most importantly, does your website have a call to action?

Your primary website can represent your practice's core values. Excellent before-and-after-photos of dental treatments are valuable for potential new patients to see and will build confidence in your ability as a dentist. Patient testimonials, photos, and statements by the doctor and the team will build confidence in the quality of your customer service. Photos of your amazing office and announcements of cool activities and upcoming events will express that a visit to your practice will be a fantastic experience.

Remember to continuously update your website. As with all printed materials, the quality of your website reflects the quality of your dental treatment. It has to be perfect.

125. EXPERTISE WEBSITE

If you have expertise in a certain aspect of dentistry, why not have a separate website dedicated to that special area? This should ensure the highest SEO (search engine optimization) for you in the search for that subject. For an orthodontist, for example, it would be ideal to have a separate Invisalign® website as the top Invisalign® provider in the dental community. This could be true for all specialists that would feature their top service whether it be implants, orthognathic surgery, root canals, or periodontal treatment, as their website. This website could also explain to the public the benefits of seeking specialty services from a specialist. If you are a general dentist, there are aspects of your practice such as CEREC, whitening, veneers, or other restorative procedures for the public is seeking an expert in that area. Be sure to post before-and-after cases and testimonials. Tailor this website to what you consider your area of expertise or the hottest feature of your clinical practice.

126. Virtual Images

The Invisalign ClinCheck is a powerful virtual marketing tool. New Invisalign patients are excited to receive and share their Invisalign ClinCheck online. They will be amazed at their predicted outcome and excited to share their set-up via e-mail with family, friends and co-workers. The Invisalign ClinCheck can be easily e-mailed as a marketing tool. Being able to see the predicted treatment result and the tray-by-tray movement of teeth will also inspire and motivate your patients throughout Invisalign treatment.

Virtual outcomes can be truly magical to restorative patients. Taking a frontal smiling photo of the patient and morphing it to show them the possibility of what their teeth could look like with a broad bright esthetic smile is powerful. For patients with skeletal discrepancies, lateral profile photos can also be morphed. We do this with the aid of Dolphin Imaging. This computer program is invaluable in making treatment decisions between treatment outcomes such as a mandibular advancement versus an upper first biscupid extraction.

Should you not have the computer technology in your practice, patient photos in new positions can be taken and shown to the patient. For example, if you have a severely retrognathic patient in need of a mandibular advancement, a lateral photo of the patient biting edge-to-edge can be shown to them as a virtual image. Similarly, someone with severe loss of vertical dimension can be asked to bite on cotton roll and a photo taken in this position to show the benefit of increased vertical height.

127. QR Code

Be sure to have an office QR code. A QR code is a small black-and-white customized computer identification print that brings patients directly to your website or Facebook page. Placing your QR code at your front desk, on all of your printed materials, and on office event announcements is a quick way for patients to connect with you and your office. Patients can click on the QR code with their smartphones and immediately be connected to your office information you wish to provide.

128. Mobile Websites, Mobile Phones

In 2013, perhaps 80% of people will use their mobile phone rather than their computer to find a new dentist or new dental specialist. It is now probably more important for a dental practice to build their mobile website before building their primary website. Old websites need to be updated so that they are mobile friendly. If your website is not mobile compatible, it is probably easiest to start with a new website rather than trying to adapt the old one. It is now possible to build a responsive site for the best possible user experience adaptable to all modes of access. This technology is avaialalbe at Sesame Communications.

Similarly, patients would probably prefer to receive text message reminders of their dental appointments on their mobile phone rather than via a reminder call. Other forms of mobile website marketing can be put in place in your office, including use of a QR code for easy social media and website access.

By giving people the power to share,
we're making the world more transparent.
–Mark Zuckerberg

The Big 3

In my world, when it comes to social media, the big three are Facebook, Twitter and LinkedIn. These sites add value to the dentist, dental office, and dental office marketing. Being connected adds value to the dentist's general education by access to dental blogs and webinars. Participating in social media will expand the dentist's community to the entire dental world. When I think back to all that I have learned from the Internet over the past several years, the new contacts that I've made, the new meetings I've attended, the new courses I've taken, and the new ideas and projects that developed, I can only conclude that it has been time extremely well spent.

129. FACEBOOK PROFILE

A Facebook profile is a human being, you. People who like you on Facebook, give you a thumbs up, are more likely to think of you when looking for your services. People may like to to find out more about you and receive updates and news about you. You are your brand, especially on Facebook.

Facebook is a vehicle to help create a relationship and ongoing communication with your patients and other dental professionals, as well as friends and family. Your content will inspire others to know you, care about you and visit your office. Share the health benefits of your services as well as some personal news. Share stories of your patients. Put the idea of your dental office in people's mind.

Think of your facebook profile as your very personal website. Post information that will establish trust and credibility. Facebook is a platform to gain permission to connect with people. You also need a Facebook Profile page to be able to respond to patient comments on your business Facebook Page.

130. FACEBOOK PAGES

Your office Facebook Page is a window into your dental office. Facebook Pages is your dental practice brand platform. Once connected, you have the ability to communicate with your Facebook patient fans via updates that appear on their homepage when they log onto Facebook. You then have the ability to engage your patients in honest communication. These genuine interactions are another way to show your patients that you care about them.

Your patients who like you on your Facebook page will become brand advocates and word-of-Facebook marketers for your dental practice. All you have to do is get the party going. By posting your patient's photos, you are encouraging them to share this photo with others and tell family and friends about your dental office. By "friending" your patients on Facebook, you also become part of their inner circle. Your fans will support your efforts and pass you along to family and friends are in need of your services. If you take time to comment on inquiries and post updates, your fans will feel as if they are part of your office brand, too.

By having your Facebook page QR code at your front desk, you can encourage patients to check in on Facebook. This can also be placed on the back of your business card and on all printed promotional material. Your e-mail response and website can also have a link to your Facebook page.

Gorczyca Orthodontics has been fortunate to receive new patients via Facebook. In 2012, I once asked a room of 500 orthodontic team members and orthodontists at the AAO annual session how many have had an iPad 2 Facebook contest. Approximately 250 hands went up. When I asked how many received a new patient from their contest, only one hand went up! Contests on Facebook are popular and increase patient engagement, which is a good thing. Contests on Facebook might increase your fan count, but they may not give you new patients quickly. Be patient. Be sure to review details of Facebook contest rules at www.facebook.com/promotions_guidelines.php.

New patients may look at your Facebook page rather than your website and make the decision to come to your office. Facebook is important. It will help you build relationships, gain information, give you leads and new contacts. It also can express that you are a friendly and fun office, and that you care about your patients.

Be sure to ask each patient and get parental consent for those under 18 years of age before posting on Facebook. We include the use of patient photos for educational purposes and social media in our initial informed consent. We never post last names and ask the patient what they would like to say. Many patients decline. That is their right. Also, we do not post anything clinical, so as not to violate HIPAA.

Your office Facebook Page will take some time thought. Multiple administrators within your office can be set up to manage this page. The answer is affirmative. Be aware, short-term profits are rare. Social media marketing is a long-term commitment and will have success in the long run.

131. Google Maps – Facebook Places

How will happy new patients find your office once they have been referred by family and friends? New patients will probably find your office through Google Maps or Facebook Places. Facebook Places has also introduced Facebook "Deals" so businesses can offer discounts, promotions and bonuses to people that check-in at their offices.

132. Reputation Monitor by 1-800-DENTIST

You may currently have no social media program in your office. Maybe you don't even know where to start. After you set up your office personal Facebook profile and office Facebook Page, Google Maps, and Facebook Places, I recommend getting Reputation Monitor® by 1-800-DENTIST. This service will identify every Internet site where your office can be listed. Reputation Monitor allows you to easily update these listings with accurate contact information, hours of operation, dental services, and your personalized commentary on what makes you and your office remarkable. The data entry will take some time, but it will be well worth it.

1-800-DENTIST has many cutting edge internet products including PatientProducer, PatientActivator, ReputationMonitor, WebDirector, and Reactivator. Take time to familiarize yourself with these products to learn more about which may help you accomplish your internet patient communication goals.

133. Google – Yelp

Do you have reviews on Yelp? Yelp is the most popular feedback system for dental patient reviews. Should you have a happy patient, a raving fan, who compliments your office and thanks you for the fine dental treatment you have done, or for the great office experience you have given them, ask them to give you a five-star review on Yelp. *Tell them* their *five-star review* would mean a lot to you. Reviews must always be done from the patient's home and never from your office. Let patients know that you are on Yelp and that you would love and appreciate a five-star review.

Should you receive a surprisingly less-than-five-star review, respond to it immediately in the best, most professional manner that reflects your clinical excellence, outstanding customer service and great patient experience that you provide. Reply only once. Perhaps 10% of reviews on Yelp are false. If you get a false review, it is important to point that out to the public in a very nice way by adding "We are having trouble finding you in our system."

134. Google AdWords and Google+

It is possible for you to enhance your presence on the Internet. This can be done by purchasing Google AdWords. Words for purchase include the name of your city, dentistry, implants, veneers, braces, Invisalign, orthodontics and orthodontist to name a few. You can test the effectiveness of your keywords by buying them and having a small Google AdWords campaign to see which words are most commonly searched. These words will be embedded in different pages on your website. This will help you appear on the first page of search results.

It has been reported that the return on investment (ROI) from the right Internet marketing campaign is greater than that of most traditional marketing projects. The number one factor in search engine optimization (SEO) is the keywords you choose to optimize. The more you use these key words, the higher your site will appear in a Google search. It has been recommended that whatever postings you make, make them on Google+ first for maximum SEO to be placed at the top of the Google search list. It's great to be seen on the first page list, especially if you're number one.

Google+ is a social media site run by Google. It is quite similar to Facebook. One helpful feature is that fans can be categorized into distinct circles of friends. Also available are hangouts or video chats with friends by invitation only. Google+ connects with all Google tools, including Google Talk. All public posts are indexed in Google's search engine, which is helpful for SEO status.

135. YouTube

Tell the truth, make a video, change the world. Better yet, let your patients make the video and talk about your dental office. These days, more videos are uploaded to YouTube in one month than the three largest broadcast networks could create in 60 years. Videocasts and podcasts offer a way to create buzz about your dental office without spending much money.

Videos can be produced in an amateur fashion in-office by iPhone or webcam to directly capture your message. You can consider hosting a patient testimonial YouTube contest. Patient testimonials and insanely great videos can be posted on your YouTube site. YouTube can turn you and your patients into Internet stars. On YouTube, anyone can upload videos for the world to see.

Kids love YouTube. My seven-year-old son searches and enjoys YouTube videos on his favorite subjects, mostly LEGOs and Super Mario. One day he found one of my office videos. "Mom, you're on YouTube!?" He was thrilled. Imagine how incredible your patient will feel to be in one of your YouTube videos. If you're an orthodontist or a pediatric dentist, why not go to where your patients are? YouTube has several hundred million views per day. Chances are your young patients are there.

136. LinkedIn

LinkedIn is a professional site where dentists, orthodontists or other dental specialists can be listed. New patients can use LinkedIn to look up the doctor and review their credentials prior to making a treatment decision.

LinkedIn can be integrated with Twitter and Blog import. The more often you update your status with business information, the more likely your contacts will notice you. LinkedIn is also for professionals to meet, to be discovered, to be included, and to build trusted connections.

137. Foursquare

Foursquare is a location-based social network that allows users to "check in" using their mobile phones at local businesses. Patients and parents in your practice can register that they are indeed at your office using

Foursquare. The Explore button shows recommended places based on their popularity among your friends and in your city. The Trending tab tells you which venues are popular based on the number of check-ins. Once a patient has checked in at your office more times over a 60-day period than anyone else, they are crowned the mayor. This participation spreads the word about your office throughout the community. Who is the mayor of your office? I think they deserve a prize!

138. TWITTER

Twitter is like a mini blogging service where you are limited to 140 characters per message, or *tweet*. It can be used both for marketing to patients, community and referring doctors, and for professional development. You can tweet about dental procedures offered in your office or about patients you've treated or anything you would like. If you use Twitter for marketing to patients, you will need to address your patient audience directly. This may enable you to connect with your ideal patient provided that your ideal patient is on Twitter looking for a dentist.

Twitter wasn't built as an engagement platform for people to connect with their customers; it was built for people to connect with each other, learn what people are doing and broadcast their own activities. For your office to participate meaningfully, they must add value to the experience. Through this, you will connect with people with similar interests.

Twitter will enable you to find people who similarly tweet about subjects in which you're interested like dentistry, orthodontics or marketing. Twitter is a valuable resource in terms of accessing marketing ideas and interacting with other dental health and business professionals. Need ideas about marketing? Just type in #dentalmarketing or #marketing and see what comes up. Twitter presents keywords such as #dentistry, #orthodontics or #marketing. Twitter allows you to connect with marketing guru Seth Godin within seconds by entering a few key words, Seth Godin, to find @ThisIsSethsBlog.

Participation on Twitter will aid you in your area of dental expertise. Twitter, just like blogs, can be used to demonstrate your expertise through value postings. You can write a note of value and link it to an article on the web that you find interesting. Twitter allows you to tell the world about your products and services. Twitter can also enable you to share a little bit of your personal life and insight. Twitter gives you a platform to interact with your community, patients, referring doctors, and other professionals with whom you share common interests.

You can respond to anyone on Twitter by using @username (@your-name). If you tweet, everyone in your network will be notified. It's viral.

A word of caution on Twitter updates: Don't update too much at a time or too often per day. Perhaps limit updates to a few per day. Otherwise, you may become too noisy and may be deleted by followers. Also, try to keep personal conversations on Twitter private if it has no relevance to the rest of the world.

139. BLOGS

Blogs are a wonderful way of expressing what you, your practice and business are all about. Here you can tell your office story. In one short essay, you can tell the world about your patient experience, dental services, team, doctor and your experience. Your office blog is a site that can be updated weekly or even daily with your personal brand story. Blogs can be used to share best practices and to reinforce core values. They can create trust and credibility.

You can write blogs about your patients, results, products, team, community activities, personal experiences or anything you would like. Everyone loves a story. This will spread your dental office name through the community and maximize your search engine optimization (SEO). The general public will receive information about your office. Blogs can also be posted on Twitter or Facebook. These links can be set up by a company named My Social Practice (www.mysocialpractice.com). This company also provides dentists with a weekly dental or orthodontic blog that is informative, entertaining and always remarkable.

On the Internet, there are many dental blogs that are extremely useful to dentists. One dental blog I love to follow is from Dr. Lee Ann Brady. Dr. Brady shares ideas about ideal dentistry and functional occlusion. She often talks about consultants, business ideas, CE classes, teamwork and many other aspects of dentistry. Another great dental blog is GoAsk-Fred, the blog of 1-800-DENTIST. Here, author Fred Joyal shares many dental marketing ideas and industry news. The Takacs Learning Center weekly blog and podcast are like a dental *People* magazine of the dental world. Here, you can learn interesting and diverse information about people, businesses, and products in the dental industry as well as gain useful practice management tips from the host himself, Mr. Gary Takacs.

140. SHARETHIS

If you are going to have a blog, it is important to have a "share this" option at the end so that your entries can be shared on Facebook, Twitter and Google+. Once installed, with the click of a button, visitors can share your blog entries with their social networks and social media connections. This makes it easy for fans, patients and other doctors to spread the name of your office and discuss what you have to share with the dental community.

141. SOCIAL MEDIA MOUSE PADS

For a bit of social media ephemera, once you have established your social media programs, custom signature mouse pads with the symbols of your programs is a possible object of announcing that news. You can give these mouse pads to all of your referring offices, businesses or patients. This useful item reminds your colleagues of your sites and lives on in the offices of your referring dentists and colleagues as a constant reminder that you are there to serve them and their patients who can also interact with you and your office on social media.

Chapter 9

EXPERIENCE

Smile at a stranger. See what happens.
−Patti LuPone

How will you bring the community into your dental practice and bring your dental practice into the community? Show up at public events and get involved. When it comes to public relations, you want your community to know who you are, trust you, engage with you, socialize with you, be delighted by you, know your story and tell others about you and the excellent life-changing dental care that you provide.

People prefer to do business with people they know and like. They also appreciate doing business with socially conscientious colleagues. It is easier to prove conscientiousness with your good deeds and actions than with your words. Community involvement gives you this opportunity.

ACTIVITIES

142. TOYS FOR TOTS

Christmas should be a wonderful time of year for children. At this time of year, engage your patients, community and referring dental offices with a Toys for Tots drive sponsored by your office and the U. S. Marine Corps. This is a campaign to collect toys for children of needy families in your community. Gorczyca Orthodontics has been involved with this program for many years. We have received bountiful donations as well as recognition for these efforts from patients, parents, the dental community and the city at large.

143. Relay for Life

We have all lost loved ones to cancer. My dear mother was taken by an ovarian-like cancer at age 71. A great way to remember those who have fought cancer is to participate in a neighborhood Relay for Life sponsored by the American Cancer Society. Many communities have a Relay for Life walkathon. This 24-hour event raises money and awareness for cancer and cancer research. Your office can participate and gain sponsors to raise money for cancer research. You may want to start your own team, get a team uniform and invite patients and their parents and friends to join. Or, you may join another large local group looking for additional members. Donation of raffle items is also accepted by Relay for Life. It is rewarding to know that your involvement and fundraising efforts are supporting finding a cure for cancer.

144. Scout Activities

Did you know there is a Boy Scout Dentistry Badge? For this badge, scouts have to study tooth structure, write about the causes of dental decay, arrange an educational visit to a dentist's office, make dental casts, get familiar with dental instruments and write an essay. You can participate in helping your patients and community scouts in the fulfillment of this badge.

There is also a Girl Scout marketing badge! With this badge, Cadettes create a strong marketing message for their annual cookie sale, learn about brand identity, research the competition, develop a marketing message and create a marketing campaign. I wish they had this badge when I was a girl!

Should a Boy Scout or Girl Scout come to your office in their uniform for their dental appointment, give them something from your office for their entire troop and invite them to an event in your office planned especially for them. Encourage them to complete their badges with your guidance. You can also host other fun activities for Boy Scout or Girl

Scout troops. These could include an Easter Egg Hunt, plaster hand cast party, oral hygiene instructions or description of how radiographs are taken, made, and interpreted.

EVENTS

145. SAFETY FAIRS AND MOUTHGUARDS

Public safety fairs through your municipal services or local dental society are an effective way to help and serve the public. Many communities have safety fairs hosted by the fire and police departments. Safety fairs are a place where the dentist can participate with a mouthguard and dental trauma safety display.

Mouthguards can also be promoted with local baseball, football or basketball teams in your community, as well as at local middle schools and high schools. Get to know the coaches at the local high schools and invite the teams to come to your dental office for a free mouthguard examination or a mouthguard program. Send schools mouthguard and dental trauma information, and offer to be available in the case of student dental trauma in your community.

146. BRIDAL FAIRS

Brides and grooms want straight, white teeth on their wedding day! When considering who demands short-term orthodontic treatment or immediate dental cosmetic tune-up, engaged couples are at the top of the list. Working closely with an excellent restorative dentist, this service can be provided by an orthodontist usually in less than six months.

Bridal fairs are also an excellent venue for distribution of orthodontic and restorative dental services information. Participation in local bridal fairs will get your office involved with the bridal business community serving brides and grooms. Invite engaged couples for dental examinations and offer them a whitening program. It is rewarding to get the future bride and groom smiles ready for their big day with beautiful straight, white teeth.

INVITATIONS

147. ACCEPT INVITATIONS

Should you be invited to a local event to participate as a sponsor or a VIP guest, accept. Your patients will be thrilled to have you in the audience. They will be happy to introduce you to their group, club, cast members, family and friends. When you attend, take time to focus on everyone you meet and those around you. Friendly introductions at events are valuable word-of-mouth referrals. People check with friends before patronizing a business.

My fondest memories of my years as an orthodontist are attending the performances of my outstanding and talented patients. One of my patients was a concerto saxophone soloist with the Oakland Symphony. Another patient was Dorothy in the play, *The Wizard of Oz*, at her middle school. Once I was invited to a birthday party. It was a cookout in the patient's backyard. I went. I had a wonderful time socializing with my patient, her friends and all of the parents. It was so thoughtful of this family to think of me and to extend an invitation.

148. GIVE INVITATIONS

When you host an office event or patient appreciation party, mail printed invitations widely to those in the community. Invite all dental society members as well as a variety of businesses, clubs, and organizations. These could include banks, Chambers of Commerce, the Rotary, accountants, landlords, the press, insurance agents, grocery stores, daycare centers, postal workers, UPS workers, gardeners, plumbers, electricians, doctors, pharmacists and nurses. Be sure to get your family and dental team involved in helping to spread the word about your office and your event.

149. SALONS AND SPAS

Salons and spas are important community crossroads. When salon owners and employees sample your dental services, they will give you valuable, free word-of-mouth marketing with all their customers.

Should you have a special event, such as an Invisalign Day, why not invite local salons and spas? If you have a special cosmetic product, such as Opalescence TresWhite by Ultradent, why not tell salons and spas about it? To learn more about spa possibilities, visit the Gorczyca Orthodontics blog http://gorczycaorthodonticsblog.com/2012/09/treswhiten-teeth/.

150. NETWORKING

Networking is your big chance to collect business cards, ask questions, listen and focus on the problems of the people you meet. Networking success is determined by how many business cards you collect, not how many you give out.

It is said that the king of networking is former President Bill Clinton. Since his time as a Rhodes Scholar in England, he has been known to have collected thousand of business cards and to write three notes about each person he meets on the back of each card. Years later, when he plans to meet someone again, he prepares by reviewing their card, remembers them fondly, and together recounts one of their special memories. This is a powerful way to be gladly accepted into the hearts and minds of those you meet.

Parents, especially mothers, are the most vocal, word-of-mouth marketing tool that you have at your disposal. Take time to personally get to know the parents of your patients and to develop and ongoing relationship with them. What percent of word of mouth do you think happens on-line? Keller and Fay in their book *The Face-to-Face Book: Why Real Relationships Rule in a Digital Marketplace* state that the number is actually only 7%. That means that the vast majority of word of mouth is still done face-to-face in person. Your exchange of stories will give you social influence. You will also have the chance to learn about wonderful marketing ideas from those you speak with including opportunity for participation in events happening in your town where you practice dentistry.

The public relations aspect of marketing includes community relations, publicity, speaking at clubs and organizations, and a variety of civic activities. All public relations activities should be reviewed for trust, ethics, credibility and social consciousness. Bad publicity is harmful to your marketing goals. Be selective in the public relations in which you participate. Avoid adverse publicity and unfavorable associations at all costs.

Do not accept new patients who are public relations hazards waiting to happen. These include patients you sense cannot be pleased by any dentist, anywhere, anytime, in any way. Beware of patients who have seen multiple dentists in the last year. Ask them why they left the previous dentist and listen to what they have to say. If it does not sound like the type of response with which you would like to be associated, do not accept this new patient. Accept new patients who will be public relations assets, who speak positively, and who you can delight and make happy.

Part Three

RELATIONSHIPS

Any time you interact with someone else,
You've initiated a relationship with that person.
Not just the first time. Any time.

–Dr. Wayne D Pernell

When it comes to referring doctors and relationship marketing, five keywords come to mind: educate, communicate, participate, produce and thank. All of these aspects of relationship marketing are important. Not every idea in these final chapters will appeal to all of your referring doctors. It is your job to find the preferences of referring doctors and build your relationship with them, one practitioner at a time.

Education is a good place to start relationship marketing. Education is the key to success. Expanding the referring doctor acumen about the services you provide will help them to recognize the need for your unique services in dentistry so that that they can more readily and easily refer to your office. This is true for all dentists and physicians referring to all other dentists and physicians.

Communicating regularly regarding the treatment of your common patients will first and foremost enhance the excellence of your clinical results and the quality of comprehensive care that your patients receive and it can also be a wonderful practice booster. An important goal is to establish excellent and frequent open communication with all referring and partner offices.

Participating in dental meetings, study clubs and local dental community social events builds strong referral relationships. Make it a goal to know each dental and medical colleague well, and to know their team personally. Participate in local study groups, continuing education events and dental societies in your community.

Producing excellent clinical results is a team effort. Patients like being treated by doctors who are interdisciplinary team members, who know each other, like each other, work well together, and produce excellent results. Your respect and enthusiasm for the doctors with whom you work is reflected by your actions and words to the patient. Enthusiasm will lead to better interdisciplinary teamwork and communication, producing a higher degree of case acceptance and patient happiness.

It is important to give thanks frequently and fervently throughout the year to referring doctors and to their entire teams. Appoint a Director of Public Relations team member for a scheduled and coordinated relationship-marketing program for your office. Never underestimate the effectiveness of thanking your doctors and expressing acknowledgement, appreciation, kindness and love.

Chapter 10

EDUCATE

Education is learning
what you didn't even know you didn't know.
–Daniel Boorstin

Education is powerful. Education in your relationship-marketing mix can include continuing education courses, display books, and written materials. If you are a dental specialist, be sure to review high quality specialty results with dentists in your community. If you are a general dentist, review your comprehensive dental care outcomes with your specialists. Education will increase diagnostic acumen, which will lead to the best comprehensive interdisciplinary treatment plan possible for your patient.

CONTINUING EDUCATION COURSES

151. CONTINUING EDUCATION PROVIDER

In California and many other states, dentists and dental specialists can become CE providers. Giving CE courses allows you to educate the dental community as well as give CE credits to all in attendance, including your own dental team. The CE provider state licenses can be attained through your state dental board. Submit your course title and course outline to the state dental board. Once a license is acquired, the dental professional can offer CE units for the courses provided. These

CE units are much appreciated by referring doctors and assistants in your community.

Giving CE courses provides the practitioner with the opportunity to present the topic and services in which they excel. It is an opportunity to educate the dental, medical and local community on dental diagnosis, treatment planning, procedures and outcomes. Giving CE courses can take your area of expertise to the next level and also be a great way to socialize in addition to getting your message of ideal dental health across. CE courses can be provided in the dental office or at a local hospital, golf club, or other conference venue.

152. LOCAL HOSPITALS

Your local hospital can be a valuable source of new patient referrals. The dentist or dental specialist can give grand rounds at a local hospital, or speak directly to oral surgery, general medicine, or pediatric departments. For instance, if you have a special interest in orthognathic surgery, let the oral surgery department know that you are available to share your experience with these cases. In addition to oral surgeons, many hospitals now also have general dentists, periodontists and other specialists on staff. Take the time to visit your local hospital and share your dental knowledge with your local medical community.

153. PEDIATRICIANS

Pediatricians are important members of your dental health team. They should be visited and educated about your dental and orthodontic services just as all your referring dental and medical colleagues are visited and educated. Pediatricians need to be made aware of early oral health concerns, including malocclusion in young children age seven and under, tongue-tie, thick maxillary frenum attachments, general oral hygiene, and prolonged thumb sucking.

154. PHYSICIANS

Plastic surgeons, dermatologists, otolaryngologists, internists, cardiologists, and orthopaedic surgeons should all be included on the dental referral list. These physicians are a powerful source of patient referrals. These physicians also work with dentists and oral surgeons on complex trauma cases and difficult third molar extractions. Physicians also need to be made aware of systemic dental concerns such as gingivitis and periodontal disease and their implications for heart disease and general health.

155. LUNCH AND LEARN

The dentist or dental specialist can host a lunch-and-learn seminar in their office and speak to colleagues and their dental teams about a variety of topics, including the art and science of dentistry and business management concepts. The hosting dentist can also provide a guest speaker for such an event.

Lunch-and-learn seminars are most successful when planned with a single office, for an extended lunch period. We have found such seminars with CE credits to be very popular and better attended in the evening hours than at the lunch hour. The host office provides food while the speaker shares information. This informal setting is very interactive and a great way to impart the latest in dental education.

156. GUEST SPEAKER

Social media is a very popular topic for peer educational efforts. The dentist or specialist may decide to bring in a guest speaker. You may also sponsor a general dentist speaker, or another specialist speaker, a dental consultant, an author, a dental accountant or a dental industry presenter. It is often possible to partner with a dental company that will provide one of these speakers free of charge.

157. PHOTOGRAPHY STUDY CLUB

Orthodontists take excellent intraoral and extraoral dental photographs. Dental colleagues often struggle with dental photography because they do not receive the same education and training in dental photography orthodontists do. A popular course provided annually by Gorczyca Orthodontics has been a Photography Study Club Hands-On Course.

Dental offices sign up individually for a one-on-one photography training session. Our records coordinator and assistants work with each dental team photographer to educate them in retractor placement, mirror selection and placement, mirror fog elimination, patient mouth opening and tongue placement, and digital photography cropping. Referring practices greatly appreciate assistance with dental photography. By providing this course, not only do you build goodwill amongst colleagues, but you will raise the level of both photographic improvement resulting in dental treatment acceptance and excellence in dental patient care.

158. Team Day Continuing Education

Your office may want to provide a Team Day Continuing Education for all your referring offices. It may be possible to partner with a company for such an event. Gorczyca Orthodontics has joined with Ultradent to provide a guest speaker, Sherri Kay, a hygienist from ACT Dental Consulting for a special half-day Team Day CE course. Sherri Kay speaks about many topics of general dental interest in developing a thriving practice, as well as many excellent Ultradent products and orthodontic cases.

Written Materials

159. Orthognathic Surgery Brochures

Orthognathic surgery and similar brochures published by Krames Publishing are an excellent patient and doctor educational referral resource. These particular brochures review all orthognathic surgical procedures, including mandibular advancement and setback, maxillary impaction, genioplasty, and surgical treatment of asymmetry. These brochures can be widely distributed and reviewed regularly with dentists, physicians and patients.

160. Bite Down Early Brochures

The American Association of Orthodontists and ADA-accredited residency-trained orthodontists recommend that all children have an orthodontic examination with an orthodontist by age seven. Bite

Down Early brochures are available from the California Association of Orthodontists (CAO). This beautiful brochure displays diagrams demonstrating seven types of malocclusions seen in children at age seven that can be corrected early by orthodontic treatment. Early treatment of these malocclusions can often prevent more severe malocclusion from developing at a later age. These brochures are great for distribution to referring dentists, pediatric dentists, pediatricians and physicians, as well as being a valuable resource for explaining malocclusions to children and their families.

161. INTERESTING ARTICLES

Send interesting articles to referring dentists and medical colleagues in your community. Share useful clinical information openly. This will enhance referrals with respect to the condition discussed. One such favored article is "Congenitally Missing Maxillary Lateral Incisors: Canine Substitution." Bjorn U. Zachrisson et al. Am J Orthod Dentofacial Orthop. 2011; 139; 434-45. This is a great summary of the dental health benefits of maxillary canine substitution of congenitally missing laterals in young patients.

162. PROMOTIONAL FOLDER

Should you meet with a referring dentist, specialist or physician colleague for lunch, come prepared with a promotional packet, display book or charts of the patients you would like to discuss. Make your meeting productive, make it educational and make it social. Have your promotional folders pre-assembled, including brochures, referral pads, business cards, invitations to events, and educational materials, such as surgery brochures, Bite Down Early brochures and interesting articles. Never come to a meeting empty-handed. Small talk should revolve around your guest, not about you. Ask them about themselves, their family or their hobbies and interests. It's *not* about you! Focus on them.

Don't say it, prove it.

–Harry Beckwith

DISPLAY BOOKS

163. DISPLAY BOOKS—ORTHOGNATHIC SURGERY

I don't think there is any patient more happy or grateful for their orthodontic treatment than an orthognathic surgery patient. At this time in dental history, there is no need for patients to live with a compromised orthodontic result or occlusal disease. We have all the tools at our disposal to fully help our patients achieve ideal occlusion. The key to achieving this result in adults often includes orthognathic surgery.

Display books are a great way to demonstrate the excellence and benefits of treatment results, especially the incredible facial esthetic and occlusal changes achieved by orthognathic surgery. By displaying before-and-after photos of the types of facial skeletal changes available to dental patients, you provide the material to promote this treatment. Without a doubt, orthognathic surgery, in conjunction with orthodontics, is a life-changing patient experience. The physical and emotional benefits of the results of orthognathic surgery dramatically improve patients' self–confidence, which may have a positive emotional impact on their lives.

Once a dentist has an orthognathic surgery display book, they will know that openbites can be corrected through orthognathic surgery. Orthognathic surgery is accessible to all patients who need it through a knowledgeable and experienced orthodontist. In California, Kaiser HMO patients have 100% coverage for orthognathic surgery. Patients who do not have Kaiser insurance usually find that their insurance will pay close to, if not 100%, of surgery costs at a university medical center.

It is also important to relay the truth regarding orthognathic surgery to the general public and dentists. Orthognathic surgery now is accomplished with rigid fixation, permanent plates that firmly hold the surgical result immediately after surgery. This procedure became available in the 1980s eliminating the need for the jaws to be wired shut.

Also, mandibular advancement patients need not stay overnight in the hospital. They return home that day and have a speedy recovery, similar to having wisdom teeth removed. A maxillary procedure may require a two night hospital stay but often, one night is sufficient.

Orthognathic surgery is an important treatment modality and needs to be emphasized with all general dentists, dental specialists and physicians. The results are extremely beneficial not only for facial esthetics but more importantly for function. Often, orthognathic surgery is the only way ideal occlusion can be achieved and occlusal disease eliminated. The general public can be made aware of the benefits and possibilities of this type of surgery. An orthognathic surgery display book and lectures as well as patient videos are wonderful tools to build awareness in your community of what you can contribute to multidisciplinary care.

164. Interdisciplinary Treatment – Display Book: Implants, Veneers, Restorative Treatment

Young patients with agenesis of permanent teeth need to be aware of implant treatment as well as the possibility of canine replacement of missing lateral maxillary incisors. Final treatment result photos are very important for the restorative dentist. Interdisciplinary treatment display books are very helpful for all dentists. These books can be made by the orthodontist who has many excellent examples of completed cases with implants, veneers, lateral restorative build-up and canine reshaping replacement of missing maxillary lateral incisors.

165. Periodontal Treatment – Display Book: Elimination of Crowding, Uprighting and Intrusion, Root Placement and Soft-tissue Procedures

Periodontists are able to refer many patients who would benefit from orthodontic treatment and restorative treatment. A periodontal display book showing periodontal health improvement after comprehensive orthodontic and restorative treatment would help the periodontist tremendously with the explanation of the benefits of comprehensive interdisciplinary cure to new patients. A picture tells a thousand words. Once periodontal patients see the results of ideal occlusion, uprighting and intrusion, tooth stability, and elimination of crowding with improved oral hygiene, they will more readily accept interdisciplinary comprehensive treatment, including periodontal procedures.

166. Orthodontic Treatment – Display Book: Extraction versus Non-extraction

The malocclusion of openbite is often created iatrogenically when teeth are not extracted for an ideal occlusal result. In my opinion, lack of anterior guidance with the need for extraction and anterior tooth retraction are the most common orthodontic clinical management errors. To achieve ideal functional occlusion, first bicuspid teeth may need to be extracted. Giving referring dentists a display book showing retreated orthodontic cases in which teeth were extracted with ideal results will increase dentist's orthodontic acumen and help them to explain to patients why orthodontic tooth extraction is sometimes necessary. Many patients who have had non-extraction orthodontic treatment, perhaps done by a non-orthodontist, may choose to return for orthodontic treatment for a second time with an orthodontist using extractions to produce a functional occlusion and esthetic facial balance.

167. Orthodontic Treatment – Display Books: Phase I Treatment, Phase II Treatment

Phase I/Phase II Early Treatment Display Books may be distributed to pediatricians and pediatric dentists, as well as to general dentists and specialists. This is a valuable tool for explaining how early treatment at age seven can prevent a more complicated malocclusion from developing, and how early arch expansion may prevent the need for tooth extraction.

The Phase I Treatment Book can include resolution of functional shifts in the primary dentition, serial extraction procedures, holding arches, and fixed retention. Phase II Treatment Books are useful in displaying the relatively mild Phase II malocclusion to be treated at age

12 after Phase I treatment, as compared to first-time comprehensive treatment at age 12.

Of course, all of the display books are extremely useful for the dentist and the treatment coordinator when encountering new exam patients and their families.

Chapter 11

COMMUNICATE

Trust is the glue of life.
It's the most essential ingredient in effective communication.
It's the foundational principle that holds all relationships.
—Stephen Covey

There are many forms of communication with our referring dentists and physicians, including verbal, written and electronic. When it comes to building professional relationships, verbal communication, in person, eye-to-eye, is perhaps the best form. Personal verbal communication conveying caring and kindness is the key to relationship success. It can be as simple as asking the question, "How are you doing?" and then listening. Listening is not a passive thing. It is perhaps the most important communication skill of all.

There can never be too much communication between doctors. Frequent and accurate communication provides a high quality of patient care. Patient information is best communicated in written form as a permanent record of the case history. This can be done via paper letters and reports. Internet and e-mail have removed the physical costs of communication and made instant exchange of information possible. Voice communications are moving more on to the Internet.

Verbal Communication

168. Phone Calls

With whom do you need to talk? Who do you need to call? With whom do you need to communicate? Think like the FBI. Would you like to have someone refer patients to your office? Call them. A phone call only takes a few minutes and a friendly "Hello, how are you?" is always appreciated. Even for your best referrers, familiarity cannot breed apathy. Reach out and touch someone you have not talked to in a while with a phone call. Try calling 10 colleagues and catching up with their lives. It only takes a minute. Listen. See what happens.

169. Case Review

The best form of communication is eye-to-eye, face-to-face, direct contact between you and your referring dentist. The best way to improve case acumen with a dental colleague is in- person, by case review. Take time to review new patient records and treatment plans with your team of referring dentists. This will help all dentists, and especially the patient, to understand the case presentation and goals, leading to acceptance of complex interdisciplinary plans.

If you have an interesting case with an impressive outcome, frame it and give the case to the referring office with whom you worked, along with a note of thanks for the referral. The referring office will proudly display the case and put it in their office with your brochures. New patients with the same problem can be shown your case results and how their problem can be similarly solved.

Written Communication

170. Reports and Letters

Throughout care, written communication between dental team members regarding patient progress in the form of an interdisciplinary letter or e-mail is very much appreciated by the partnering dentists. All practitioners involved can be continuously updated. Written communication from the orthodontist can include the initial exam letter, the start of orthodontics letter, a copy of initial records (including Panoramic radiograph, cephalometric radiograph, tracings and photos), a progress letter, a progress Panorex, and a completion letter, with copies of the final records and recommendations for final restorations.

General dentists have always complimented our office for our progress letters sent one year in orthodontics and on our evaluation of hygiene and third-molar development. This open communication is a good way to update progress and to check on hygiene status, as well as follow up on regular cleaning appointments.

171. Fax

Faxes are great for patient treatment communication between offices. Faxes are a timely and cost-effective means of recorded communication. Faxes will be immediately seen by front desk team members, whereas e-mails may not be read for hours or even days, and snail mail letters may remain on the doctor's desk unopened in a stack for days. In addition, should you be hosting an event, faxes can also be used to confirm the event date and time, as well as manage RSVPs.

172. Cards

Sending a card or postcard of thanks and good wishes to your referring doctors is a nice thing to do. Examples include a photo Christmas card, a New Year's wish or calendar, a Happy Thanksgiving card, a Thank-you card, or a Valentine postcard that reads, "We love our referring dentists." Photo cards, which are inexpensive and easy to make, allow your referring offices to have a visual picture of the voice on the other end of the phone. This card will probably be hung or displayed in the referring dentist's office. This thoughtful act of sending a card will keep you in the hearts and minds of referring dentists and other healthcare providers.

ONLINE COMMUNICATION

173. ONLINE RECORDS

Sesame Communications and TeleVox offer online record access to your patients and to the referring doctor 24/7. You and your dental colleagues can share photos and radiographs of your patients. Each dentist needs to choose a password for the Sesame Communication System, and be shown how to use the log-in. Once this is done, access to the mutual patient records will be an easy and efficient paperless system.

174. STATE-OF-THE-OFFICE ADDRESS

Dental offices can write and send a state-of-the-office letter annually to referring doctors and patients. This can be done in the first quarter to discuss what is new in the office. Topics can include new technology, new team members, new events and new procedures offered. The newsletter can also highlight some of the personal achievements of the doctor and the team, as well as continuing education courses attended. It is also a great way to start off the New Year. Your "state-of-the-office address" can be e-mailed, mailed, included in a newsletter or even posted as a blog.

Chapter 12

PARTICIPATE

To find out what one is fitted to do,
and to secure an opportunity to do it,
is the key to happiness.

−John Dewey

Participation is marketing. If you are engaged and involved within the dental community, marketing and public relations are happening whether you know it or not. In their book, *Putting the Public Back in Public Relations,* Brian Solis and Deirdre Breakenridge discuss the language of the new PR. They state that in the new social world, PR is about dialogue, a two-way discussion that brings people together to discover and share information, either over the Internet or in person, face to face.

However you participate in spreading your message of your office and your dental services, with whomever and wherever you meet, come prepared. Have photos, articles or printed materials with the name of your office and information about you and your services in your possession for immediate delivery. Be involved in spreading the good news about your dental office and dental procedures, and be enthusiastic, friendly, knowledgeable and available. Participate!

175. SEATTLE STUDY CLUB

Involvement in a Seattle Study Club (SSC) is an educational, social and rewarding career experience. Seattle Study Club is a national organization with regional study-club components. Participation in your local community Seattle Study Club allows general dentists and specialists to work closely and well together on the treatment planning of complex comprehensive interdisciplinary restorative cases. By this process, all participating dentists have the opportunity to learn about techniques and procedures that restorative dentists, periodontists, endodontists, prosthodontists, oral pathologists, oral surgeons and orthodontists provide. The educational program is extremely broad-based, spanning every aspect of dentistry and areas of medicine, pharmacology and dental practice management. It is also possible for the general dentist or specialist to be a speaker at the local Seattle Study Club meeting or at the annual national Seattle Study Club conference. If you do not have a Seattle Study Club in your area, you may want to start your own.

Study clubs are a wonderful way to participate in excellent comprehensive patient care, and receive CE credit. Other study clubs may be combined with the Seattle Study Club. At Gorczyca Orthodontics, we have also had an in-office study club to discuss orthodontic treatment specifically. We have hosted an Invisalign Study Club. Hosting and participating in such dental study clubs will only make your daily practice of dentistry more enjoyable and fulfilling.

176. American Association of Dental Office Managers

The American Association of Dental Office Managers (AADOM) is a national organization that promotes education in dental office management to dental office managers, team members and dentists. The AADOM has a Fellowship Program that your dental office manager can fulfill by taking valuable management classes online. The AADOM national annual meeting is a great place to hear excellent dental practice management speakers. It is a meeting that the office manager, dentist and other team members can attend.

The Northern California AADOM chapter meets four times per year. We discuss dental office management topics such as marketing, teamwork, treatment coordination, customer service, management systems and human resource management. You can also have guest speakers. AADOM is a great way for team members from different offices to get to know each other, help each other and share practice management tips and ideas.

If you do not have a local chapter of AADOM, you may want to become a founder. You can get the information online at www.dental-managers.com.

177. BUSINESS INFORMATION

Pass along valuable business education with your referring dental colleagues. You are in the dental business and you can help another doctor with what you have learned about business management.

Updates of the office manual and annual changes to employment law can be shared regularly with fellow dentists. Gorczyca Orthodontics works with Barbara Freet of Human Resource Advisors, Lafayette, California to update our team manual each and every year. Another helpful resource is HR for Health at www.hrforhealth.com/. This is important information that needs to be shared. We have also brought in excellent business management guest speakers. One has been accountant Jay Wirig of Thomas, Wirig, Doll CPAs, of Walnut Creek, California. This talk was about dental office embezzlement, which has been known to affect nearly half of all dental offices. The McGill Advisory Newsletter also contains timely knowledge and advice. A subscription to this newsletter can even be given as a Christmas gift to referring offices.

Chapter 13

GIVE

Giving is better than receiving
because giving starts the receiving process.

−Jim Rohn

If you want to get, you've got to give. Your office can be a giving place. When it comes to dental relationships, it is helpful to give time, adventure, recognition and gifts. If you give a gift, make it memorable in its thoughtfulness and presentation. Give your doctors consistent service. Give commitment to your doctors with your support through thick and thin.

TIME

178. PAID POSTAGE

Paid return postage on your referral pads will help your colleagues refer to you conveniently and efficiently, at no cost to them. This will facilitate the prompt placement of the referral card in the mail by the referring doctor and team. Having the new patient's home phone, cell phone and e-mail address included on the referral pad allows you to call the new patient even if they have not yet called you. This is a great level of customer service that you can provide to both the referring doctor and the patient.

179. Lunch

Why not mix business with pleasure? Enrich your life with the interesting people who make up the dental profession in your local community. It's natural to meet with people and everyone needs to eat. Lunch is a wonderful way of getting to know your dental colleagues with whom you have so much in common.

When it comes to business, you're not at lunch to eat. A lunch meeting is a business meeting. You do business at business meetings. Don't waste valuable time making a lengthy lunch selection. Don't ask the waitress for special favors. Your friend is your focus, not your food.

As an orthodontic specialist, I go out to lunch with a referring dentist almost every day. Nothing can beat personal interaction. If you are dedicated to getting to know your fellow dentists, never eat alone. You can schedule a one-and-a-half-hour lunch each day. Drive to the restaurant, eat and drive back to the office in time for your next after-lunch patient.

To save time, open an account at your local favorite restaurant. If seating is tight, ask for a reserved table. Order one course that is quick to eat. Come prepared. Bring pertinent office information in a welcome packet to enable you to make a quick lunchtime exit.

Arrive on time or better yet, be early. Be happy, excited and appreciative of your guest. Be cheerful and humorous. Thank them for their time. Ask your lunch guest questions about themselves, their hobbies, their family, and listen. Talk about their interests, not yours. Make a commitment to work together.

Lunch is one of my favorite marketing tools because I love meeting and getting to know people. Some dentists will be shy. They may not want to take the time to do lunch or may even be unfriendly. Never give up. Be persistent. Be patient. Don't take it personally because they may not even know you at all. It may take time, but sooner or later you will break through. You will become friends.

Be sure to introduce yourself. I once had lunch with an older pediatric dentist I had never met before. Halfway through our time together, he said to me, "When is the doctor going to get here?" I explained that I was Dr. Gorczyca and we had a laugh. After that, we became very good friends.

Doctor lunch is a wonderful way to start some great friendships and find things you have in common with others. Relationships are the spice of life. Enjoy your time together. *Bon Appétit!*

180. DINNER PARTIES

Can't do lunch? Well, how about dinner? Dinner can be either at your home or at a restaurant. I used to host a dinner party at my home almost every Friday night. Six is the perfect number for great conversation. I would invite two dentists with their spouses. Afterward, even some of the general dentists who had never met before became good friends, joining together in disability groups and covering for each other in their offices. A dinner at a club or restaurant or perhaps even an outdoor cookout are other good ideas. It is after all the time that you spend together that counts.

ADVENTURE

Live your life allegro vivace.
–Ann Marie Gorczyca

181. THE SYMPHONY

When I was in High School, I had the incredible privilege of playing principal flute in an All New England Orchestra under the baton of Conductor Benjamin Zander. It was a life changing experience for me. Classical music is pure passion, and this is what conductor Benjamin Zander is able to express. That's the way classical music is, it expresses the sublime and touches the human soul. Wouldn't it be wonderful if we could feel this passionate about dentistry? Wouldn't it be amazing if we could express unspoken feelings of caring to our patients and touch them as human beings?

For several years, I have taken my top 10 referring doctors for a night out to the San Francisco Symphony for a concert. This is always an adventure for all of us. Several of my dental colleagues had never been to the symphony. Some had not been to an orchestral performance since they were children. Some needed to buy new suits. Some even rented limousines. It was a date night and spouses also loved it.

A night out to a moving performance will be remembered for years to come. Should you host such an event, for ease of administration I recommend getting a written RSVP card and distributing the tickets shortly before the event. Check the weekend you have selected carefully to avoid graduations, holidays and sports events such as the Super Bowl.

182. Hunting/Fishing Trip

Many male dentists love to hunt and fish. I was once honored to be invited on a fishing outing from the Berkeley Marina by an endodontic specialist. The boat left at 6:00 a.m., sailing to the open sea under the Golden Gate Bridge. It was a cold morning and the sea was rough. We fished for sea bass, salmon and haddock. I learned an important lesson that day. Men fishing don't talk. The lines were cast and we gathered as a group focused on our fishing poles. My thought was, "Is anyone going to talk?" Then it got worse. I caught the most fish. I had three within two hours when someone finally broke the silence, saying, "Hey, all the fish are going to women and children!" My secret: Let the professional on board bait the line for you. This was a wonderful event. I will always be grateful that I was invited on this remarkable adventure.

183. Afternoon Tea

By contrast, female dentists love to talk. They do this best at an afternoon tea. We talk and talk and talk. There is not much that women dentists don't share with each other. Women dentists rarely need to call for references on departed team members from a friend's dental office; we already know the information before the person has even dropped their *résumé* at our office door. An afternoon tea is a wonderful gathering that you can host at your home or at a café or restaurant. Make a few sandwiches, buy a few cakes and cookies, boil the water, and let the adventure of great conversation flow with the tea.

184. GARDEN PARTY

One thing I love to do for my dental colleagues is to host a garden party at my home at The Sea Ranch, California. This is a wonderful couple's event. The dentists and their spouses love drinking champagne and viewing the many beautiful flowers in the gardens, not to mention climbing on the rocks and exploring the beach and caves by the ocean. Added to the adventure is the breathtaking two-and-a-half-hour drive north on California Coastal Highway 1. Of course, golf is also an excellent social event, especially for men. There is a golf course at The Sea Ranch, which makes for an enjoyable alternate activity for those who love to play golf.

185. SPORTS TICKETS

Go Giants!!! For many years, my husband was a San Francisco Giants season ticket holder. We would give tickets to our dental colleagues, business associates and patients. The most wonderful years were when the San Francisco Giants won the World Series. The excitement in Northern California was unforgettable! Season tickets to a local sports team are extremely popular. They come in handy as a quick and convenient gift. Taking someone out to the ball game is an enjoyable way to spend a sunny afternoon.

186. SPA DAY

A spa day gift certificate is a pleasurable doctor and team gift. Orthodontic and dental management consultant Rosemary Bray once told us that the gift of a spa day would feel great and be much appreciated and any and all dental offices. Gorczyca Orthodontics decided to take Rosemary's advice and give this gift as a Christmas present. She was right. In return, the thank-you notes we received from our referring dental offices were voluminous and heartfelt. Spa day was a big hit!

Massages are healthy and therapeutic for stress and muscle tension so commonly found in all dental professionals. To put together a spa day program, we recommend a 20-minute massage for each assistant and a one-hour massage for the doctor. Massage teams can be contracted by appointment to visit the dental office on a specific date and time. Some doctors prefer to receive their massage at home rather than with their team. Some dental teams made a party of their spa day. Should the spa day be scheduled on an office work day, be sure to allow time for packing up equipment before patients arrive back to the office.

187. Office Party

It is great to give an office party to get to know people and make new friends. If you give an office party, make it unique. One endodontist in our county hosts a dress-up Halloween party every year. Choosing a Halloween costume as a team each year has been a pretty cool thing. He then gives a prize for the best team costume. Gorczyca Orthodontics was happy to win first place in 2012 for our group costume "Angry Birds."

However, it is not great to have your office closed for too long to be giving a party and lose time, money and patients. I will share with you a true story about three specialty offices. One specialist's office had a party, was closed for two days and his phones were not answered. A second specialist's office, which had three specialists and three offices, gave a party around the same time. All three of their offices were closed for one day, and their phones were not answered. The third specialist's office did nothing and did not host a party. This office was available to see patients, answered the phone, gave excellent customer service to their referring offices and patients, received the referring dentists' calls and saw all referred and emergency patients. The third office got all the referrals.

This was the dental scenario relayed to me by my dental colleagues at our weekly lunch meeting. The lesson of this story is, if you are going to have a party, consider still answering the phones and serving patients and referring doctors. Consider having the party off site so that your office does not have to be closed at all, or close your office for the least amount of time possible. The purpose of your marketing is to have your phones ringing *and* answered.

RECOGNITION

Recognition is free. It costs you nothing. It is the most precious thing to the person who receives it. Acknowledgement and appreciation go a long way. Never underestimate the power of kindness and love.

188. DENTIST OF THE YEAR

"And the winner is…" Giving special recognition to the most outstanding dentists in your community can be thrilling and make the receiver feel great. Receiving Dentist of the Year Award can really make someone's day. My colleague was so excited to receive a certificate that read, "Dentist of the Year," and a gift plate that read, "You Are Special Today," that he went home and shared this with his family and children. His family was so proud of him! They thought that he was great and he is!

189. HYGIENIST OF THE YEAR

Everyone loves hygienists. Give special attention and recognition to these outstanding healthcare professionals. We do this by involving them in a special certificate program with our mutual patients mentioned earlier (see #49). We save the certificates with names and signatures and tally who is the most involved hygienist with our patients. At year-end, the one with the most signed certificates gets the special award, Hygienist of the Year.

It is always a very happy day for us to give the Hygienist of the Year award. We usually accompany this with a $100 gift certificate to Macy's or for a one-hour massage. One winner once exclaimed, "I've never won anything before. This is the happiest day of my life!"

190. CUSTOMER SERVICE AWARD

What award could be better than a customer service award given for turning patients into raving fans? If a receptionist at another dental office has given your patients outstanding customer service which your patients have told you about, let the patient coordinator know how much you appreciate them, thank them, and honor them with a Customer

Service Award. This is guaranteed to make their day. Say thank you and recognize them. Let them know how much their referrals are appreciated and how much this talented receptionist means to you.

191. Office Lunch

Having lunch is an awesome way to say thank you and let someone know that they truly matter. An office lunch with a referring office is a great way to make people happy and to spend time together. Gorczyca Orthodontics has been taken out to lunch several times by other specialists. It has meant so much to us to spend time with these offices and their wonderful teams. These lunches made us feel special. This generous gesture definitely felt great and helped us remember these thoughtful specialists.

Sending lunch to an office is appreciated and can save time. We all must eat. Everyone loves food. When given the option, never underestimate the power of lunch! It will promote communication and friendship, which will also lead to the best patient care possible.

If you are an orthodontist, pediatric dentists can be your best referral source or not, depending on whether they employ their own orthodontist. If they are your best referral source, you may want to thank them for their referrals by giving them their own lunch party. No matter what the circumstances, it pays to be nice to everyone, always. Get to know all the pediatric dentists in your community. You will be working very closely with them. Orthodontists will also have many patients without a pediatric dentist or a general dentist. Referrals go in both directions.

Gifts

Giving a dentist a gift lingers in the mind of the dentist until this dentist receives another gift from someone else. However short-lived the marketing effect, gifts are still a kind and thoughtful token of appreciation. Who doesn't love receiving a gift?

Physical gifts to referring dentists are given in friendship. It should be absolutely clear that any gift in recognition of the excellent care rendered by a dental colleague or office is independent of referrals.

Obviously, gifts cannot be given directly in return for referrals. This is not acceptable by the state board or ethically in the dental or medical profession. Should you want to give a token of appreciation, you are best to give a verbal thank you or handwritten note.

"Who sent this gift basket?" This question should never be asked about your gift. Make your office name prominent and glued onto the gift basket itself. Make the gift presentation from your office memorable. The wrapping is half the fun. Make it big and impressive. A custom-made sticker with your office logo and the message "A Gift for You From…" with your office name becomes handy for this purpose. Baskets can be made with the "A Gift for You From…" office stickers. No additional cards or writing will be needed.

192. SPARKLING WINE OR CIDER

If you are announcing the opening of a new practice, you may consider personally delivering the announcement with a referral pad to each office, along with a bottle of sparkling wine or sparkling cider. This announcement certainly will be remarkable and not casually thrown away. Celebrate with your referring dentists and let the libations flow. Sparkling wine or cider makes a great gift, which is especially appreciated and can be saved for New Year's Eve.

193. BOUQUETS

"Voilà!" said the magician as he pulled out a bouquet of flowers. Bouquets are marketing theater. Not only do they delight, smell and look beautiful, floral bouquets will sit at the front desk in a dental office for many days, be complimented, enjoyed, and be appreciated by all who sees them. A floral bouquet is an easy, convenient, cost-effective token of appreciation.

Fruit bouquets are also unique, fantastic and delicious. The company Incredible Edibles makes eye-catching fruit bouquets. Fruit is also a healthy snack. When's the last time you ate a chocolate covered strawberry?

194. FOOD

From donuts to cookies, breads to brownies, popcorn and pretzels, peaches with cream, or wine and cheese, all forms of food are appreciated. Are you hungry yet? What you like, your colleagues will like. Fruit plates and vegetable platters are appreciated by the health conscious. Be creative. See the world through the eyes and stomachs of your colleagues. Remember to think of them often and fondly with food. It's the thought that counts.

195. SAMPLER BASKETS

Surprise! Dental team members love getting surprises. One popular gift idea is to assemble a beautiful basket of small gifts such as body sprays, cosmetics and lotions, allowing each team member to choose an item that your PR director brings to their office. This form of interaction, with a friendly smile and eye-to-eye contact, an introduction by name and time to talk, produces an opportunity to create a bond of friendship.

196. CANDLES AND MATCH BOXES

Do you have match boxes from your favorite restaurants that have lasted a long time, even years? Do you even have a collection? A candle with customized match boxes from your office can make a beautiful, fragrant unique gift for a referring dental office. It's a warm touch to have a scented candle burning in your dental office on a rainy day or during the colder months of fall and winter. The aromatherapy of a candle is appealing to dental patients and calming to those treating them. In addition to lighting the office candle, everyone will use their matches to light their home candles and fireplaces so be sure to include plenty in your candle gift basket. Make the surprise gift presentation impressive with pretty wrap and a large ribbon bow. Bigger is better when it comes to presentation. Don't forget the "Special Gift For You" sticker. After the candle is burned out, your match boxes will continue to serve a useful purpose and travel far and wide.

Chapter 14

PRODUCE

There's no traffic jam on the extra mile.

–Anonymous

Do everything in your power to ensure the high quality and long-lasting features of your dental treatment, customized service and patient experience. To be successful with your dental marketing, you must offer quality dental care and service. Otherwise, even the best marketing in the world won't motivate a patient to return to your dental office more than once.

197. DIAGNOSTIC WAX-UP

The diagnostic wax-up is a study model set-up of your proposed treatment plan for the patient. The diagnostic wax-up is a must for communication of what the treatment plan will be for interdisciplinary cases involving implants and veneers with orthodontic treatment. The diagnostic wax-up can be reviewed by all dentists, as well as the patient, before the start of comprehensive treatment. This is a valuable tool in communication between all parties involved. It is beneficial for patient case acceptance for the patient to see a model of their potential, beautiful comprehensive treatment result.

198. In-bound Telemarketing

The almighty telephone can make or break the appointment of a new patient to your office. In-bound telemarketing requires excellent phone service and demeanor. Excellent phone service requires having the phone answered within the first three rings by a cheerful, friendly human. Plan to have this occur every time the phone rings within your hours of operation, including lunchtime. If you need help with phone answering during the lunch hour, after hours or during vacation weeks, you may want to consider a professional phone service such as Dental Support Specialties, LLC. They can be contacted at www.dentalsupportspecialties.com.

Dental offices can benefit by having a designated lunchtime receptionist. It is also a good idea to have an early morning "first in" receptionist who comes in before the doctor and other team members arrive, listens to all phone messages, and calls patients before the start of the busy day. Many early-morning messages will be cancellations of that day's appointments or patients wanting to get in that same day. These schedule changes need to be made before the morning huddle. You will also benefit from having a designated evening "last out" phone receptionist. Families appreciate calls in the evening hours when parents are home and able to talk about treatment or scheduling of appointments. Be sure to also have every patient's cell phone number, which is most often the contact number of choice. Patients may also request text messaging.

For ease of contact, have the doctor listed by name in the phone book. Should your office have a general name, such as Great Orthodontic Smiles, not every new patient or family will remember that, but they should remember the name of the doctor, especially if it is distinctive. Patients will tell their family and friends the name of the doctor most often when speaking about them, and new patients may look for the doctor by calling information and asking for the dentist by name. It is very important that the dentist be listed by name in the phone directory even for ease of contact with referring dentists.

199. Lights On, Doors Unlocked

It's important for your patients and referring dentists not to find themselves in need when your office door is closed and the lights are out. Your office can always be attended, lights on, doors unlocked. During normal business hours, Monday through Friday 8:30 to 5:00 p.m., patients expect offices to be open. When the doctor is not in the office, it is important for the receptionist to always continue to do his/her job in a normal function: lights on, doors unlocked. Newly referred patients and established patients with questions or problems may choose to come directly to your office. Fellow dentists need to see that you are open, too. Availability is big! Remember the three As of practice success in order of importance: Available, Affable, Able. Sometimes, the only thing you need to do to market your practice and schedule a new patient is to be open for business!

What can you do during non-business hours to help your patients? Would an after-hours phone-answering service be of value in gaining new patients? Maybe you should consider a service such as 1-800-DENTIST. Patients have diverse schedules. The dental offices that can accommodate them will win and gain new patients.

Would patients benefit from having your cell phone number or beeper to call in case of an emergency? Let new patients and your referring doctors know that when the lights are out, you want them to come back when the lights are on, and that you are willing to turn the lights on for them at any time.

200. Serve Referred Patients

Service is anything the referring dentist wants it to be. One way to achieve wonderful referrals is to do what referring dentists want you to do. This might be seeing a new patient today. It may require scheduling a new patient during lunchtime or after hours. It means going the extra mile. Listen to what your referring dentists want, and then give it to them.

When your office receives referrals, call the patient immediately to schedule the appointment, and try to get the new patient into the office within three days. Should the patient not be home the first time you call, call again, then text or e-mail again a few days later. Send a card of welcome to the new patient, and follow up with them.

In general, follow up with new patient exams one day later, one week later, one month later and one year later. If the patient was a referral, send the referring dentist a letter after one month telling them you have tried to contact their patient but have not yet been successful in scheduling the exam. Then, follow up one year later and never, ever give up. Patients do come in for their new-patient exam one year after being referred. Studies have shown that 80% of customers buy on the seventh attempt. Seven is a magic number. If you're there for the long run, committed to starting treatment because it benefits the patient, that signal needs to be sent loud and clear. Leave all new-patient information in your computer system, always assuming that the referred new patient wants to come in unless you hear definitively that they have started treatment at another office.

When you aim for the top, you make important progress
by just the aiming.

–Jon Spoelstra

201. EXCELLENCE

Whether you are a general dentist, orthodontist or other dental specialist, excellence and the conveyance of clinical excellence is the most important aspect of your marketing. Patients want value. They want quality. And above all, they want dentists they can trust. They want durability and long-term stability of their results. As a dentist, you must always strive to produce clinically excellent, ideal and long-lasting treatment. It is important also for your patients, community and referring doctors to know that you are clinically excellent.

Show your patients that you honor excellence by guaranteeing patient satisfaction. This cannot be done when putting a time limit on your services. At Gorczyca Orthodontics, we have a patient-satisfaction policy that orthodontic appliances are removed at the request of the patient who is told that their braces are ready for removal. The patient confirms in writing that they have been told that their braces are ready for removal, that they are happy with the orthodontic result and that they are requesting removal of their braces.

Put your clinical excellence on the table in the form of your plaster study models for all of the dental community to see. Present cases frequently to your patients, to the community and to your dental study clubs. In the marketplace, display your clinical excellence in the beautiful smiles that you produce.

There are many verifications of clinical excellence. If you are a general dentist, there are many academies and institutes for you to develop your clinical skills. If you are a specialist, you have specialty boards. If you are an orthodontist and have achieved clinical excellence by becoming a Diplomate of the American Board of Orthodontics, let this be known. If you are a member of other prestigious merit-based dental organizations, such as the Angle Society of Orthodontists, let people know. In 2001, when I received my Diplomate status of the American Board of Orthodontics, I printed cards announcing that I had completed this evaluation process. I sent out approximately 250 cards to every member of the Contra Costa Dental Society. The same month in return, I was amazed to receive 152 referrals. This was a wonderful token of congratulations from my dental colleagues, which I appreciated so much and will never forget.

Deliver excellence in the treatment that you provide and have your marketing reflect the excellence in your treatment. The first and last word of dental marketing is to take great care of your patients and to deliver clinical excellence.

CONCLUSION

Success is turning knowledge into positive action.
                                        –Dorothy Leeds

Clayton Christensen wrote, "When the tension is greatest and resources are most limited, people are actually a lot more open to rethinking the fundamental way they do business." Like it or not, dentists need to work a little harder these days to maintain their level of practice success or to continue to grow their practices. Marketing will help you achieve this goal.

All three parts of dental marketing that we have reviewed need thought, time and attention. An effective dental marketing management system is to create an annual calendar of the three areas of dental marketing. This calendar and a sample marketing calendar are found in the appendix of this book. Commit to one marketing event each month in each one of these three marketing category columns. Set up a 12-month marketing plan and adopt a budget. Analyze your returns, continue what works and discontinue what does not work.

Marketing budget guidelines have been set by accountants and consultants. A mature practice may have a marketing budget of 3% of revenue for practice maintenance. A 4-5% marketing budget may yield single-digit growth, whereas a 6% marketing budget may produce above 10% annual growth. Plan your marketing budget according to your practice goals.

In the words of marketing expert Seth Godin, marketing isn't expensive any longer and it takes more guts than money. The single best way to become a marketer is to market.

It is my sincerest hope that this book will help you initiate your practice marketing plan and that some of the ideas from this book implemented in your dental practice will bring joy to your patients, you and your team, and make your practice remarkable. Dentistry is a noble profession. Join me in the quest for clinical excellence, outstanding customer service and a great patient experience.

We can do no great things, only small things with great love.
–Mother Theresa

Whatever you do with marketing, it is my hope that you will do good work in the world. The key to marketing is implementation, one idea at a time, one action at a time, one day at a time. Consistency of action counts. Just get started and grow your practice. It all starts with marketing!

MARKETING CALENDAR TEMPLATE

	Patients	Community	Doctors /Team
Jan			
Feb			
Mar			
Apr			
May			
June			
July			
Aug			
Sept			
Oct			
Nov			
Dec			

Appendix 2.

SAMPLE MARKETING CALENDAR

	Patients	Community	Doctors /Team
Jan	Calendar Distribution	Community Guide	AADOM Meeting
Feb	Candy Heart Contest	Direct mail post-cards 1x, 2x April, 3x June	Chocolate Roses Valentine postcard
Mar	10 Year Retainer Check Postcards	Valpak 1x 2x Aug, 3x Nov	Doctor Lunches
Apr	Mother's Day Invisalign Promotion	In office Girl Scout Day	Team Day: Guest Speaker
May	Update Doctor Wall of Fame Family Pictures	Update Brochures	In office CE 1x, 2x, 3x, June 4x, July 5x
June	Patient Wall of Fame	H.S. Career Day Speaker	Photography Study Club
July	Patient Testimonials Summer Splash Party	Summer Splash Party	Summer Splash Party
Aug	2014 Calendar Coloring Contest 5x	Chamber of Commerce	Gift Basket Sampler
Sept	Poem	Preschools, Elementary Schools	Candles
Oct	Candy Corn Contest	Halloween Toothbrushes	Display Books
Nov	Kid's Day	Middle School Mouthguard Program	Seattle Study Club
Dec	Light-up Toothbrushes	Holy Rosary Ladies Dinner	Christmas Cards/ Gifts

ACKNOWLEDGEMENTS

Ride the crest of the wave.
—Ann Marie Gorczyca

Books are built over time. This resource has been a personal labor of love. It is the result of numerous years in clinical practice, experiences, conversations, classes, resources and collaboration among my colleagues who care about orthodontics, dentistry and marketing. Thank you to all of you for sharing your thoughts and experiences with me.

I am grateful to the people who made this book possible. Thank you to the excellent team at Gorczyca Orthodontics without whom patient care and marketing activities would not exist: Jolene, Monica, Veronica, Lyndsay, Jessica, Taylor and Tiffany.

Thank you to Marianne Way for the initial transcription of this manuscript. Thank you to Jennifer Andert of Patterson Dental for your encouragement. Thank you to Keith Wilson of Henry Schein for your advice, enthusiasm and guidance.

Thank you to John Smulo of Purple Cow Websites for his friendship and guidance with social media.

Thank you to my dear friend Dr. Maureen Valley, Orthodontic Clinic Director at the Arthur A. Dugoni School of Dentistry for organizing the Practice Management Course which gave birth to first a lecture, then a presentation, then a book.

Thank you to Fred Joyal for his friendship and inspiration in his trailblazing work in the field of dental marketing, and for writing the introduction to this book.

A special thank you to Rosemary Bray, a guiding light in orthodontics and dentistry. Your friendship, hard work, and sterling example make you a true role model for all of us.

Thank you to elite Orthodontist Dr. Neal Kravitz for his enthusiasm and high standards for dentistry and the orthodontic profession. Your contribution proves that one person can make a difference.

Thank you to Judy Kay Mausolf for her optimism, advice and support in the final stages of this book.

Thank you to Dr. Lee Ann Brady for her support and her amazing educational contributions to the dental profession. Your work in occlusion brings together all aspects of dentistry and produces clinical excellence for the maximum benefit of the patient.

Thank you to my accountant Jay Wirig for his advice that "It is impossible to do too much marketing." I have always enjoyed your fatherly guidance and emphasis on good moral values.

Thank you to my friend Patrick Schwerdtfeger and to my publisher, Stephanie Chandler of Authority Publishing, for their advice on how to write a book.

Thank you to my sister Diane Gorczyca Patrick, M.D. for her editorial skills and insight from the field of medicine.

Thank you to my husband for proofreading and final editing of this manuscript. All my love to Richard and Richard who shared with me this writing adventure every step of the way with patience, forbearance, and love.

Thank you to all of you who have purchased this book and read it to the end.

Ann Marie Gorczyca, D.M.D., M.P.H., M.S.
The Sea Ranch, California

INDEX

A

AADOM. *See* American Association of Dental Office Managers
AAO. *See* American Association of Orthodontists
Abundance, ix–x
Activities
    Girl Scout Marketing Dentistry Badge, 96
    Relay for Life, 96
    scout activities, 96–97
    Toys For Tots, 95–96
ADA. *See* American Dental Association
Adult patient, seniors day, 25
Adventure. *See also* Events
    afternoon tea, 124
    garden party, 125
    hunting, fishing trip, 124
    office party, 126
    spa day, 125–126
    sports tickets, 125
    symphony events, 123–124
Advertising Specialty Institute, 37

Affordable Image, 68
Afternoon tea, 124
Age 55+, community target markets, 74
American Association of Dental Office Managers (AADOM), 63, 118–119
American Association of Orthodontists (AAO), 73, 79, 106
American Dental Association (ADA), 81
Angle Society of Orthodontists, 135
Articles, cards, 29
Awards, 29–30

B

Beckwith, Harry, 108
Before-and-after photos, 15
Bite Down Early brochures, 106–107
Blogs, 93–94. *See also* Internet
Book donations, 59
Boorstin, Daniel, 103
Bottle water, custom-label, 37

Bouquet gifts, 129
Boy Scout Dentistry Badge, 96
Branding. *See also* Community
    target markets
  church bulletins, 69
  colors, 67
  community guide, 68
  direct-mail postcards, 68
  local arts performances, 70
  logo, 66
  magazine articles, 70
  names, naming, 65–67
  office signs, posters, banners,
    flyers, 70–71
  photos, 66–67
  radio, 72
  repetition, 66
  signs on bulletin boards, 71
  Smile of the Week, 70
  story, 67
  ValPak, 68–69
  video, 72–73
  welcome guide, 67
  The Wellness Hour, 72–73
  word of mouth (WOM), 73
  words, 67
Bridal fairs, 97
Brochure placement, community
    target markets, 75
Brushing stations, 11–12
Buffett, Warren, 43
Bulletin boards, branding, 71
Business information, participation,
    119

C
Calendars, 40–41
California Association of
    Orthodontists (CAO), 107
Candles, match box gifts, 130
Cards, postcards, 115

Care calls, 17
Care-day speaker, 59–60
Case donations, 60–61
Case review, verbal communication,
    114
Chamber of Commerce, 81
Christensen, Clayton, 137
Church bulletins, 69
City council meeting, 79–80
Civic centers, community target
    markets, 75
Class awards, 61–62
Cleanliness, 12, 30
Clinical excellence, 134–135
Clinton, Bill, 99
Colors, 67
Comfort break, 16
Communication. *See also* Verbal
    communication; Written
    communication
  Chamber of Commerce, 81
  city council meeting, 79–80
  community business network, 80
  forms of, 113
  hospitals, 81
  in-bound telemarketing, 132
  lights on, doors unlocked, 133
  patient diagnostic wax-up, 131
  Rotary Club International, 80–81
Community business network, 80
Community guide, 68
Community target markets
  age 55+, 74
  brochure placement, 75
  civic centers, 75
  ethnic groups, 74
  Halloween reverse canvassing,
    76–77
  opening day events, 75–76
  women, 74–75
Competition, xi

Complimentary, free consultation, 56–57
"Congenitally Missing Maxillary Lateral Incisors: Canine Substitution" (Zachrisson), 107
Contests, 34–35
Continuing education centers
    continuing education provider, CE courses, 103–104
    guest speaker, 105
    local hospitals, 104
    lunch-and-learn seminars, 105
    pediatricians, 104
    photography study club, 105–106
    physicians, 104–105
Covey, Stephen, 113
Customer Service Award, 127

D
Debond Day, 27–28
Dental health evangelist, 55–56
Dental marketing
    goal, xvi
    main categories, xv
Dental Support Specialties, LLC., 132
Dentist of the Year Award
    recognition, 127
Dewey, John, 117
Diagnostic wax-up, 131
Digital X-rays, technology, 11
Dinner party giving, 123
Directions, signage, 20
Direct-mail postcards, 68
Display books
    interdisciplinary treatment, 109
    orthodontic surgery, 108–109
    orthodontic treatment, 110
    periodontal treatment, 109–110
District events, schools, 63
Doctor

    smiling, 51–52
    "Wall of Fame," 9–10
Dolphin Imaging, 85
Drinkware, 41
Drucker, Peter, xvi

E
Eco-Dentistry, 42
Education, relationship marketing, 101–102
Elevator pitch, 52
Emails, 46
Ethnic groups, 74
Events
    adult patient, seniors day, 25
    bridal fairs, 97
    Debond Day, 27–28
    Halloween skating party, 24
    house calls, 24–25
    ice cream social, 23–24
    Invisalign Day, 25–26
    Kid's Day, 22–23
    new technology day, 27
    office banner, 28
    safety fairs, mouthguards, 97
    Santa Claus Party, 24
    sports tickets for, 35, 125
    Summer Splash Party, 23
    Super-Starter Day, 26–27
Everything is Marketing (Joyal), 16
Excellence, 134–135
Expertise website, 84–85
External marketing, public relations, xv
    publicity *vs.*, 53
    target marketing areas, 53–54

F
Facebook
    pages, 87–88
    profile, 87
The Face-to-Face Book: Why Real

Relationships Rule in a Digital Marketplace (Keller, Fay), 99
Faust, Mark, xvi
Fax, written communications, 115
Fay, Brad, 99
Financial arrangements
    discounts, 45
    extended payment plans, 43–44
    family plan, 45
    insurance, 44, 108
    savings, 45
    uninsured patients, 54
    0% financing, 44–45
Flat-screen announcements, 46
Fond farewell, 17
Food gifts, 130
Foursquare, 91–92
Fragrance, 14–15
Franklin, Benjamin, xi
Free consultations, 56
Frisbees, 39

G
Games and movies, 8
Garden party, 125
Gates, Bill, 83
Gifts, 32
    bottle water, custom-label, 37
    bouquets, 129
    calendars, 40–41
    candles, match boxes, 130
    contests, 34–35
    custom beach balls, towels, 39
    dinner parties, 123
    drinkware, 41
    electronic toothbrush, oral
        hygiene kit, 35
    food, 129
    Frisbees, 39
    going-green tote bags, 42
    key-ring lights, 40
    light-up toothbrushes, 32

lunch, 123
paid postage, 123
patient logo T-shirts, 33–34
pens, pencils, 37–38
physical gifts, 128–129
poems, positive words, taglines,
    41–42
promotional hats, 34
referrals and, 129
refrigerator magnets, 39
sampler baskets, 130
sparkling wine, cider, 129
sports tickets, 35, 125
for team, 130
time, 121–123
tooth fairy, 36
treasure/reward chest, 36
wooden tokens, 32
wristbands, 38–39
Girl Scout Marketing Dentistry
    Badge, 96
GoAskFred, 93
Godin, Seth, 1, 138
"Going green," 42
Going-green tote bags, 42
Google AdWords, Google +, 90
Google Maps, Facebook Places, 20,
    89
Goonik, James, 53
Gorczyca, Ann, 123, 141
Graham, Katherine, 21
Guerilla Marketing (Levenson), 71, 74
Guest, Edward, 41
Guest speaker, continuing education
    centers, 105

H
Halloween
    reverse canvassing, 76–77
    skating party, 24
Hats, 34

Hospitals, 81, 104
House calls, 24–25
Hunting, fishing trips, 124
Hygienist of the Year Award, 127

I
Ice cream socials, 23–24
In-bound telemarketing, 132
Interdisciplinary treatment, display
      books, 109
Interesting articles, 107
Internal marketing, 1, xv
Internet
   blogs, 93–94
   Dolphin Imaging, 85
   expertise website, 84–85
   Facebook pages, 87–88
   Facebook profile, 87
   Foursquare, 91–92
   Google AdWords, Google +, 90
   Google Maps, Facebook Places,
      89
   Invisalign ClinCheck, 85
   LinkedIn, 91
   mobile websites, mobile phones,
      86
   My Social Practice, 93
   primary website, 83–84
   QR code, 85–86, 88
   Reputation Monitor®,
      1-800-DENTIST, 89
   search engine optimization
      (SEO), 84, 91, 93
   ShareThis, 94
   social media mouse pads, 94
   Takacs Learning Center, 94
   Twitter, 92–93
   virtual images, 85
   Yelp reviews, 89–90
Invisalign ClinCheck, 85
Invisalign Day, 25–26

Invitations
   accepting, 98
   giving, 98
   networking, 99–100
   salons, spas, 98–99

J
Janitorial services, 12
Joyal, Fred, 16, 93–94, ix–x
Junior college teacher, schools, 63

K
Keep in touch, 31
Keller, Ed, 99
Kerpen, Dave, 22
Keurig® beverage maker, 7–8
Key-ring lights, 40
Kids
   daycare center, 57–58
   elementary school, 58
   Frisbees for, 39
   middle schools, 59–60
   movies and games for, 8
   pillow pets for, 14
   stuffed animals for, 14
   treasure/reward chest for, 36
   wooden tokens for, 32
   wristbands, 38
Kid's Club, 16
Kid's Day, 22–23
Kotter, Phil, 153

L
Labeling, 9
Leeds, Dorothy, 137
Levenson, Conrad, 71, 74
Lights on, doors unlocked, 133
Light-up toothbrushes, 32
LinkedIn, 91
Local arts performances, 70
Location, parking, 20
Logo, 66
Logo T-shirts, 33
Lunch giving, 122
Lunch-and-learn seminars, 105
LuPone, Patti, 95

M

Magazines, 8–9, 67
  articles, 70
Maister, David, 55
Marketing
  budget guidelines, 137
  learning, xi–xii
  Ps of, 1
Marketing calendar, 139–140, xvi
Mathew 17:20, 65
Mobile websites, mobile phones, 86
Mother Teresa, 138
Mouse pads, 94
Mouthguards, safety fairs, 97
Movies and games, 8
Music, 13
My Social Practice, 93

N

Names, naming, 65–67
Networking, 99–100
Nurses, 4

O

Ochs, Adolph, 68
Office
  banner, 28
  brochures, 7
  decorations, 13–14
  feeling, 3
  "going green," 42
  lights on, doors unlocked, 133
  lunch, recognition, 128
  party, 126
  signs, posters, banners, flyers,
    70–71
  state-of-the-office address, 116
  tour, 5–6
On-hold messaging, 46
Online communication
  online records, 116
  state-of-the-office address, 116
Opening-day events, community

target markets, 75–76
Oral hygiene kit, 35
Orthodontic surgery
  brochures, 106
  display books, 108–109
Orthodontic treatment
  display books, 110

P

Paid postage giving, 123
Paradise Dental Supplies, 32
Parent Teacher Association (PTA),
  62–63
Participation
  American Association of
    Dental Office Managers
    (AADOM), 63, 118–119
  business information, 119
  Seattle Study Club, 117–118
Patients
  comfort, 16–17
  diagnostic wax-up, 131
  experience, xii
  feedback, 17
  happiness of, 5, xii
  logo T-shirts, 33–34
  models of clinical excellence, 4–5
  referrals, 5
  restroom, 12
  satisfaction policy, 134–135
  satisfaction survey, 18
  testimonials, 18–19
  trust, 15
  uninsured, 54
  "Wall of Fame," 10–11
  we will take great care of you, 3–4
Pediatricians, continuing education
  centers, 104
Pens, pencils, 37–38
Periodontal treatment, display
  books, 109–110

Pernell, Wayne, 101
Peters, Tom, xv
Phone calls, verbal communication, 114
Phone service, 132
Photography study club, continuing education centers, 105–106
Photos, 15, 66–67
Physicians, continuing education centers, 104–105
Pillow pets, 14
Poems, positive words, taglines, 41–42
Posters, 14
Primary website, 83–84
Principle for the Day, 61
Products, 21
Professional dress, demeanor, 48–50
Promotion
    elevator pitch, 52
    emails, 46
    excellent team attitude, 48
    professional dress, demeanor, 48–50
    smiling doctor, friendly team, 51–52
    team business cards, 50–51
    team code of business etiquette, 50
    thanks, 46–47
Promotional folders, 107–108
Promotional hats, 34
PTA. See Parent Teacher Association
Public relations. See also External marketing; External marketing, public relations defined, 54
Purple Cow (Godin), 1
Putting the Public Back in Public Relations (Solis, Breakenridge), 117

Q
QR code, 85–86, 88

R
Radio, 72
Reception area, 13
Recognition
    articles, cards, 29
    awards, 29–30
    children's patient recognition, 29
    Customer Service Award, 127
    Dentist of the Year Award, 127
    hygiene certificates, 30
    Hygienist of the Year Award, 127
    keep in touch, 31
    office lunch, 128
    personalize thank-you notes, 28–29
    10 year retainer check, 30–31
Referrals, 5, 18, 30, 31, 129, 133–134
Refreshments, 7–8
Refrigerator magnets, 39
Relationship marketing, xv
    education, 101–102
    team and, 101–102
Relay for Life, 96
Repetition, 66
Reports, letters, written communication, 114–115
Reputation Monitor®, 1-800-DENTIST, 89
Rotary Club International, 80–81

S
Safety fairs, mouthguards, 97
Salons, spas, 98–99
Sampler basket gifts, 130
Santa Claus Party, 24

Schools
    book donations, 59
    care-day speaker, 59–60
    case donations, 60–61
    class award, 61–62
    daycare centers, 57–58
    district events, 63
    elementary schools, 58
    junior college teacher, 63
    middle schools, 59–60
    Parent Teacher Association
        (PTA), 62–63
    Principal for the Day, 61
    visitors, 60
Scout activities, 97
Search engine optimization (SEO),
    84, 91, 93
Seating for family and friends, 12
Seattle Study Club (SSC), 117–118
SEO. *See* Search engine optimization
Sesame Communications, 116
ShareThis, 94
Signage, directions, 20
Signs on bulletin boards, 71
Smile of the Week, 70
Social media mouse pads, 94
Solis, Brian, 117
Spa day, 125–126
Sparkling wine, cider gifts, 129
Specialists, 4
Spoelstra, Jon, 134
Sports tickets, 125
State-of-the-office address, 116
Story, 67
Stuffed animals, 14
Sugiyama, Raymond, 30
Summer Splash Party, 23
Super-Starter Day, 26–27
Symphony events, 123–124

T
Takacs Learning Center, 94
"Take Home a Smile" (Guest), 41
Team
    business cards, 50–51
    code of business etiquette, 50
    excellent attitude, 48
    friendly, 51–52
    gifts for, 130
    relationship marketing and,
        101–102
    training, 10, 119
    "Wall of Fame," 9
Technology. *See also* Internet
    digital x-rays, 11
    new technology day, 27
TeleVox, 116
10 year retainer check, 30–31
Thanks, 46–47
Thank-you notes, 17–18, 28–29
@ThisIsSethsBlog, 1
Tooth fairy, 36
Tote bags, 42
Toys For Tots, 95–96
Treasure/reward chest for, 36
Twitter, 92–93

U
Ultradent, 12
Uninsured patients, 54

V
ValPak, 68–69
Verbal communication
    case review, 114
    phone calls, 114
Video, 72–73
Virtual images, 85
Visitors, 60

W

Warm welcome, 6
Websites. *See* Internet
Welcome folder, 7
Welcome guide, 67
The Wellness Hour, 72–73
Whitening, 12
Wilde, Oscar, 66
WOM. *See* Word of mouth
Women, 74–75
Wooden tokens, 32
Word of mouth (WOM), 73
Words, 67
Wristbands, 38–39
Written communication
    cards, postcards, 115
    fax, 115
    reports, letters, 114–115
Written materials
    Bite Down Early brochures,
        106–107
    "Congenitally Missing Maxillary
        Lateral Incisors:
        Canine Substitution"
        (Zachrisson), 107
    interesting articles, 107
    orthodontic surgery brochures,
        106
    promotional folder, 107–108

X

X-rays, technology, 11

Y

Yelp reviews, 89–90

Z

Zachrisson, Bjorn, 107
Zander, Benjamin, 123
Zuckerberg, Mark, 86

ABOUT THE AUTHOR

Marketing takes a day to learn.
... it takes a lifetime to master.

–Phil Kotter

Dr. Ann Marie Gorczyca is a Clinical Adjunct Professor of Orthodontics at the Arthur A. Dugoni School of Dentistry University of the Pacific, where she teaches practice management. Marketing is the first lecture of a six-part series that she gives including marketing, teamwork, treatment coordination, customer service, systems management and human resource management.

Dr. Gorczyca is a Diplomate of the American Board of Orthodontics, member of the Angle Society of Orthodontists, and graduate of Advanced Education in Orthodontics (Roth course). She is a member of the Seattle Study Club (SSC), the American Association of Orthodontists (AAO), the Pacific Coast Society of Orthodontists (PCSO), the California Association of Orthodontists (CAO), the American Dental Association (ADA), the California Dental Association (CDA), and the Contra Costa Dental Society. She was an orthodontic associate of Dr. T. M. Graber in Evanston, Illinois. She has worked in a multispecialty group practice in Fairfield, California, and she has been in her solo private practice as an orthodontist in Antioch, California for almost 20 years.

Dr. Gorczyca graduated from Wellesley College, Harvard School of Dental Medicine, Harvard School of Public Health and Northwestern University. She has studied marketing at the Harvard School of Public Health, Department of Health Management and Policy, as well as at

153

Stanford University and San Francisco City College. She is the founder of the American Association of Dental Office Managers (AADOM) East Contra Costa County study club. She has also served on the AAO Council of Communications and ADA National Boards Part II Test Construction Committee.

Dr. Gorczyca was a marketing speaker at the 2011 and 2012 American Association of Orthodontists Annual Sessions.

She lives in Walnut Creek and The Sea Ranch, California with her husband and son. This is her first book.

BIBLIOGRAPHY

Bailey, Maria T. *Marketing to Moms.* Roseville, California, Prima Publishing, 2002.

Beckwith, Harry, and Clifford, Christine K. *You, Inc.* New York, Business Plus, 2007.

Beckwith, Harry. *Selling the Invisible: A Field Guide to Modern Marketing.* New York, Business Plus, 1997.

Beckwith, Harry. *What Clients Love.* New York, Business Plus, 2003.

Berger, Jonah. *Contagious.* New York, Simon & Schuster, 2013.

Brogen, Chris, Smith, Julien. *The Impact Equation.* New York, Portfolio/Penguin, 2012.

Carnegie, Dale. *How to Win Friends and Influence People.* New York, Pocket Books, 1982.

Carter, Brian *The Like Economy.* Indianapolis , Que Publishing, 2012.

Christensen, Clayton M., *How Will You Measure Your Life?* New York, Harper Collins Publishers, 2012.

Cooper, Frank. *The Customer Signs Your Paycheck.* New York, McGraw Hill, 2010.

Covey, Stephen R. *The 7 Habits of Highly Effective People: Powerful Lessons in Personal Change.* New York, Free Press, 2004.

Edward, Nark. R., Ewen, Ann J. *360 Degree Feedback,* New York, Amacom 1996.

Faust, Mark. *Growth or Bust* Pompton Plains, N.J., Career Press 2011.

Flynn, Anthony, Vencat, Emily Flynn. *Custom Nation,* Dallas, BenBella, 2012.

Fox, Jeffrey. *How to Become a Rainmaker.* New York, Hyperion, 2000.

Gehrt, Jennifer, Moffitt, Colleen. *Strategic Public Relations 10 Principles to Harness the Power of PR.* U.S.A., Xlibris, 2009.

Gitomer, Jeffrey. *Little Gold Book of Yes Attitude.* Upper Saddle River, New Jersey, FT Press, 2007.

Godin, Seth. *All Marketers Tell Stories.* New York, Penguin Group, 2009.

Godin, Seth. *the dip.* New York, Penguin Group, 2007.

Godin, Seth. *Purple Cow.* New York, Penguin Group, 2002.

Godin, Seth. *Whatcha Gonna Do With That Duck?* New York, Penguin Group, 2012

Goolnik, James. *Brush.* London, Bow Lane Limited, 2011.

Hsieh, Tony. *Delivering Happiness -A Path to Profits, Passion, and Purpose.* New York, Business Plus, 2010.

Joyal, Fred. *Everything is Marketing.* Los Angeles, Futuredontics, 2012.

Keller, Ed, Fay, Brad. *The Face-to-Face Book.* New York, Free Press, 2012

Kennedy, Daniel S. *The Ultimate Marketing Plan.* Holbrook, MA, Adams Media Corporation, 1991.

Kerpen, Dave. *The Likable Business.* New York, McGraw Hill 2013.

LeBoeuf, Michael. *How to Win Customers & Keep Them For Life.* New York, Berkley Books, 1987.

Levinson, Jay Conrad. *Guerilla Marketing- Easy and Inexpensive Strategies for Making Big Profits from Your Small Business.* Boston, Houghton Mifflin Company, 2007.

Levinson, Jay Conrad, McLaughlin, Michael W. *Guerilla Marketing for Consultants.* Hoboken, New Jersey, Wiley, 2005.

Levinson, Jay Conrad, Gibson Shane. *Guerilla Social Media Marketing.* USA Entrepreneur Press, 2010.

Miles, Linda. *Dynamic Dentistry.* Virginia Beach, Virginia, Link Publishing, 2003.

Miletsky, Jay. *101 Ways to Successfully Market Yourself.* Australia, Course Technology, 2010.

Peters, Tom, Austin, Nancy. *A Passion for Excellence, the Leadership Difference.* New York, Grand Central Publishing, 1986.

Peters, Tom. *The Little BIG Things.* New York, HarperCollins Publishers, 2010.

Pink, Daniel H. *To Sell is Human.* New York, Penguin Group, 2012.

Rosen, Emanuel. *the anatomy of buzz- how to create word of mouth marketing.* New York, Portfolio/Penquin, 2012.

Schwerdtfeger, Patrick. *Make Yourself Useful.* Austin, Texas, Bard Press, 2010.

Schwerdtfeger, Patrick. *Marketing Shortcuts for the Self-Employed.* Hoboken, New Jersey, Wiley, 2011.

Singh, Shiv and Diamond, Stephanie. *Social Media Marketing for Dummies.* Hoboken, New Jersey. John Wiley & Sons, 2012.

Solis, Brian, Breakenridge, Deirdre. *Putting the Public Back in Public Relations.* Upper Saddle River, New Jersey, Pearson Education, 2009.

Spoelstra, Jon. *Marketing Outrageously Redux How to Increase Your Revenue by Staggering Amounts!* Austin, Texas, Bard Press, 2010.

Takacs, Gary. *The Thriving Dentist's Show.* Takacs Learning Center, Podcast, 2011-2013.

Tapscott et al. *Digital Capital: Harnessing the Power of Business Webs.* Boston, Harvard Business School Press, 2000.

Timm, Paul R. *50 Powerful Ways to Win New Customers.* Franklin Lakes, New Jersey Career Press, 1997.

Wheeler, Alina. *Designing Brand Identity.* Hoboken, John Wiley & Sons, Inc., 2013

Wilson, Jerry R. *151 Quick Ideas to Get New Customers.* Franklin Lakes, New Jersey, Career Press, 2005.

CPSIA information can be obtained
at www.ICGtesting.com
Printed in the USA
BVOW11*2104250517

485064BV00010B/114/P